THE FINANCIAL PEACE PLANNER

Dave Ramsey is a personal money management expert, an extremely popular national radio personality, and the author of the *New York Times* bestsellers *The Total Money Makeover*, *Financial Peace Revisited*, and *More Than Enough*. In these books Ramsey teaches others how to be financially responsible, so they can acquire enough wealth to take care of loved ones, live prosperously into old age, and give generously to others.

Ramsey knows first-hand what financial peace means in his own life—living a true riches-to-rags-to-riches story. By age twenty-six he had established a four-million-dollar real estate portfolio, only to lose it by age thirty. He has since rebuilt his financial life and now devotes himself full-time to helping ordinary people understand the forces behind their financial distress and how to set things right—financially, emotionally, and spiritually.

Ramsey offers life-changing financial advice as host of a nationally syndicated radio program, *The Dave Ramsey Show*, which is heard by more than two million listeners each week, on more than two hundred radio stations throughout the United States.

Ramsey is the creator of Financial Peace University (FPU), a thirteen-week program that helps people dump their debt, get control of their money, and learn new behaviors around money that are founded on commitment and accountability. More than 100,000 families have attended FPU classes at their workplace, church, military base, local nonprofit organization, Spanish organization, or community group, and many national corporations have used and benefited from the program as well. The average family pays off $5,300 in debt and saves $2,700 in the first ninety-one days after beginning FPU and is completely out of debt, except for the mortage, in eighteen to twenty-four months.

Ramsey created a group of products in an effort to teach children about money before they have a chance to make mistakes. Financial Peace for the Next Generation is an all inclusive school curriculum that is currently used in more than three hundred schools across the country. Financial Peace Jr. is an instructional kit designed to help parents teach their young children about working, saving, and giving their money. Through Ramsey's entertaining four book series, *The Super Red Racer*, *Careless at the Carnival*, *The Big Birthday Surprise*, and *My Fantastic Fieldtrip*, children learn about working, saving, giving, and budgeting.

Ramsey earned his B.S. degree in Financial and Real Estate from the University of Tennessee. A frequent speaker around the country at large-scale live events, Ramsey is a passionate and inspiring presenter who is at ease on both sides of the mike. Hundreds of thousands of people have dramatically changed their lives using Ramsey's seven baby steps to financial peace.

He resides with his wife Sharon and their three children, Denise, Rachel, and Daniel, in Nashville, Tennessee.

Dave Ramsey

The Financial *Peace* Planner

A STEP-BY-STEP GUIDE
TO RESTORING YOUR FAMILY'S
FINANCIAL HEALTH

PENGUIN BOOKS

PENGUIN BOOKS

Published by the Penguin Group

Penguin Group (USA) Inc., 375 Hudson Street, New York, New York 10014, U.S.A.

Penguin Group (Canada), 90 Eglinton Avenue East, Suite 700, Toronto,
Ontario, Canada M4P 2Y3 (a division of Pearson Penguin Canada Inc.)

Penguin Books Ltd, 80 Strand, London WC2R 0RL, England

Penguin Ireland, 25 St Stephen's Green, Dublin 2, Ireland (a division of Penguin Books Ltd)

Penguin Group (Australia), 250 Camberwell Road, Camberwell,
Victoria 3124, Australia (a division of Pearson Australia Group Pty Ltd)

Penguin Books India Pvt Ltd, 11 Community Centre, Panchsheel Park, New Delhi – 110 017, India

Penguin Group (NZ), 67 Apollo Drive, Rosedale, North Shore 0632, New Zealand
(a division of Pearson New Zealand Ltd)

Penguin Books (South Africa) (Pty) Ltd, 24 Sturdee Avenue,
Rosebank, Johannesburg 2196, South Africa

Penguin Books Ltd, Registered Offices: 80 Strand, London WC2R 0RL, England

First published in Penguin Books 1998

50 49 48 47 46 45 44 43

A NOTE TO THE READER
This publication is designed to provide accurate and authoritative information
with regard to the subject matter covered. It is sold with the understanding that
the publisher is not engaged in rendering financial, accounting, or other professional advice.
If financial advice or other expert professional assistance is required, the services
of a competent professional person should be sought.

ISBN 978-0-14-026468-5

Printed in the United States of America
Set in New Caledonia
Designed by Vicky Hartman

To all the Financial Peace University members
who have fought the good fight against
financial stagnation and devastation and,
in the end, committed to be something other than normal

Acknowledgments

IT TAKES THE WORK of many people to complete a book, and to everyone who played a part in the writing of *The Financial Peace Planner*, I wish to extend my gratitude. In particular, I want to thank Susan Salmon Trotman and Jane von Mehren: You have helped me capture on paper some of life's most important principles. Thanks to Sara Fortenberry, who helped me learn the ropes of publishing. And as always, I thank God for my beautiful wife, Sharon, and our three children. These principles wouldn't mean nearly as much had my family not stayed committed to me throughout all of life's hard lessons.

Contents

Contents

Part III · Watch Your Wealth Grow

The Financial *Peace* Planner

Part 1

Where Are You Really?

ONE

Call Me Weird— Just Don't Call Me Broke

KIT NERVOUSLY LOOKED around the room as she introduced herself to the fifteen people attending the financial counseling seminar with her. "I always paid our bills on time and watched my spending when I was married," she said. "I'm not really sure why things changed after the divorce—I thought I was making pretty good money for someone who hadn't worked in years. But no matter how much I tried to save during the past two years, I just kept sinking a little deeper and a little deeper into debt."

Sitting next to her, Barry nodded. "We knew we were in trouble, but we had no idea how bad it was until collectors started calling. Emily and I just looked at each other like, 'How did that happen?'"

It's a common cry among people who seek financial counseling: How did that happen? One day everything seems fine; the next day you wake up in debt. I've got news for you: It didn't happen overnight. It took a while for you to rack up that $30,000-plus of debt. You just weren't paying attention while it added up. And I've got some more news for you: You are going to learn to pay closer attention than you ever have to what you spend and why you spend it. Over the past ten years, I have come to see that financial management is 80 percent behavior and 20 percent know-how. Whether it's bad behavior or lack of know-how that got you into trouble, the Financial Peace program will help you correct both. You will get out of debt, stay out of debt, and take control of your financial life. Not only will you be able to have the life you want, you'll also be able to retire with dignity and leave a legacy of financial good health to future generations.

Let's start by looking at the 80 percent, your behavior. In the list that follows, check the statements that are true about you:

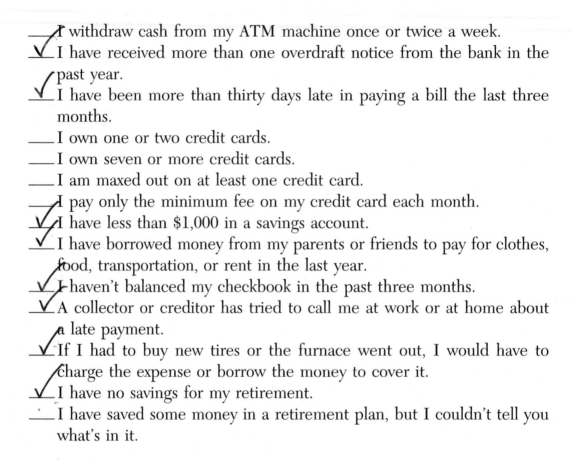

____ I withdraw cash from my ATM machine once or twice a week.
__✓__ I have received more than one overdraft notice from the bank in the past year.
__✓__ I have been more than thirty days late in paying a bill the last three months.
____ I own one or two credit cards.
____ I own seven or more credit cards.
____ I am maxed out on at least one credit card.
____ I pay only the minimum fee on my credit card each month.
__✓__ I have less than $1,000 in a savings account.
__✓__ I have borrowed money from my parents or friends to pay for clothes, food, transportation, or rent in the last year.
__✓__ I haven't balanced my checkbook in the past three months.
__✓__ A collector or creditor has tried to call me at work or at home about a late payment.
__✓__ If I had to buy new tires or the furnace went out, I would have to charge the expense or borrow the money to cover it.
__✓__ I have no savings for my retirement.
____ I have saved some money in a retirement plan, but I couldn't tell you what's in it.

For every statement you checked, give yourself two points; then, add your total points and find what your score means below:

0–4 points: The Get-Aheads

You are starting to make it. You have money left over each month after paying bills, but probably you aren't sure how to invest it. Sometimes you can't explain where the money has gone and you find yourself saying things like, "With what we make and spend, we should be able to save more." With a few tips and some self-control, you will soon see your money explode into wealth.

6–10 points: The Currents

You are living on the edge. You bring home the bacon each month, and you send it right back out. You have never been late on a payment, but you can't save. So college, retirement, and major purchases all loom as debt looking to happen.

12–20 points: The Troubled

Until that unexpected event a few months ago, you were a Current. Now, you are in over your head. You are thirty to sixty days delinquent on your credit cards or house or car payments, and you have begun to get nasty calls. You have considered debt consolidation or other borrowing tactics just to catch up. Stop! It *is* time to get serious about your debt, but you won't pay it off overnight. Slow down. If you make the right choices now, you can recover financially with little or no damage to your credit.

22–28 points: The Desperadoes

You are probably close to giving up. You have thought about the B word (bankruptcy) and possibly discussed it with your spouse or friend. Foaming-mouthed collection monsters call your home every night during supper to threaten foreclosure on your home (if it's not already there). You are several months behind on your car payments, making repossession imminent. Even so, credit bureaus are the least of your worries. You would settle for relief from the unending fear and strain.

Wherever you are on this scale, there is hope. Whether you haven't learned how to save or can't figure out how to pay off your debt, I can assure you it doesn't take a rocket scientist to manage money well. On the contrary, during the past ten years as I have counseled people on my call-in radio show, *The Money Game*, at my Financial Peace seminars, and in my office, I have witnessed hundreds of people walk out of financial crisis and onto the road to financial peace by applying the simple principles taught in this workbook.

Unfortunately, carrying debt is considered "normal" in America. According to *The Consumer Reports Money Book*, the typical American household carries an average debt of $38,000. Seventy percent of Americans live paycheck to paycheck, says a *Wall Street Journal* study. And the 1996 National Foundation for Consumer Credit survey shows that 90 percent of Americans worry about paying their bills. That doesn't mean we are bad people. It does mean we have lost control.

Somewhere along the way, we missed out on an important financial principle: *Money is active.* It grows or shrinks depending on whether you save or spend. If you save and invest your money well, time and interest rates will help it grow. You can save $10,000 in a 12-percent-interest-bearing account for ten years and it will grow to $31,100. On the other hand, if you choose to borrow and spend, time and interest rates will cause you to lose money. For example, you can buy $10,000 worth of stuff, using a 12-percent-interest credit card, and wind up paying approximately $12,300 (if you pay only the monthly minimums).

The bottom line is you have to gain control over your money *before it controls you.* You have to make your money work *for* you instead of *against* you. You want to *own* rather than *owe*.

"Money doesn't control me," you say. Really? Which of the following are true of you?

_____I was late to an appointment because I was trying to clear up a credit problem.

✓ I have had trouble getting to sleep more than once in the last week because I was thinking about money.

_____(*For those in denial*) I have had trouble getting to sleep lately and it *could* be because of money.

_____I was late to an appointment or missed a deadline because I had to spend time at the bank, clearing up some overdraft charges.

——I spent more than three hours trying to balance my checkbook last month.

——I have made a significant purchase—$300 or more—that my spouse doesn't know about yet.

——My spouse is mad at me because I made a significant purchase without telling him/her.

✓I don't answer the phone at night, for fear it's a collector.

——My spouse and I fight frequently about finances.

If you checked any of the above statements, you have lost control of your money. The next twelve chapters will help you get it back. First, you will examine where you are financially and how you got there so you keep from doing it again (chapter 2). Then, you will focus on regaining control of your finances through budgeting, implementing the envelope spending system, and using the "debt snowball" to deliberately repay what you owe (chapters 3–6). You will learn negotiating techniques to help you start living within your means and how to clean up your credit report (chapter 7). Then, you'll learn how to make your money work for you through saving, investing, and growing your wealth so you can accomplish long-term goals of retirement, college planning, and home ownership (chapters 8–13). The process will take time. But remember, you didn't get into debt overnight. You won't get out of debt and on the road to fiscal fitness overnight either.

Nor can you expect to get the full impact of the lessons in this planner if you whiz through it in one or two days. You will need to read each chapter carefully, paying attention to "Wake-up Calls," which will help move you to action. Questions and exercises throughout help you evaluate your spending and saving habits. And from time to time, you will be challenged to take one of what I call the "seven financial baby steps":

1. Save $1,000 in an emergency fund.
2. Pay off all your debt except the mortgage using the debt snowball.
3. Complete your emergency fund by saving three to six months' expenses.

4. Fully fund your pretax retirement savings.
5. Save for your kids' college.
6. Pay off your home early.
7. Build wealth and give like crazy!

Named for the *Baby Steps* book Richard Dreyfuss's character writes in the movie *What About Bob?*, these steps are the bedrock of the Financial Peace philosophy. Skip or fudge on a step, and you are likely to wind up back where you are now. That's why there are "Baby Step Checkups" in the "Peace Track" sections at the end of every chapter. You should use these to record your progress and set goals for how you will complete each step. In addition to the Baby Step Checkups, the Peace Track sections include personal goal-setting charts and other exercises to keep you thinking. Use all of these tools and apply them to your own financial situation.

Wake-up Call!

It is imperative that the whole family be involved in this process. It won't help for you to improve your financial habits if the rest of the family doesn't change with you. If you are married, you and your spouse need to do the exercises in this book, as well as the budgeting, planning, eliminating debt, and saving together. If you have children, don't be afraid to explain to them what's going on. For children under ten, you may want to use some discretion; but if you are in deep financial trouble and about to lose your house, for example, you will have to be honest. Remember to keep it simple: "Daddy and Mommy made some mistakes with their money and now we are going to have to move." Teenagers can handle more; in fact, they respond surprisingly well to parents who are honest about their failures, as long as they are not made to feel that they caused the problems.

Give yourself a week to complete each chapter, but don't be surprised if it takes longer than fifteen weeks to really change your habits. Many folks read my book *Financial Peace*, attend the twelve-week financial boot camp, Financial Peace University, and spend time coming to the office for individual counseling before they start conquering some of the habits that got them into trouble in the first place.

One warning: It isn't normal in America to live debt-free and save your money for the future. So, as you do the exercises in this planner and start changing, some people will call you weird. Big hairy deal! What would you rather be, broke or weird? When you are out of debt and sitting on a million dollars in mutual funds, the people who think you are weird will be crawling to you for help. Then you can see who's weird.

First Things First

When one area of your life gets out of balance, it's easy to let the others go too. You can become so afraid you won't be able to pay bills that you forget to pray or exercise. You may spend so much time working to get out of debt that you forget to take much-needed breaks to be with your wife or husband or children.

Before you move on to chapter 2 and start tackling the hard work of getting your finances in order, take time to order the rest of your personal life.

- **Spiritually:** Spend time every morning quietly thinking about the day or rededicating your life to the Lord. Ask yourself, What are my goals for the day? What is one thing I can do today to improve my financial fitness? Try to have a pen or pencil and paper handy so you can jot notes to yourself. Perhaps you will want to keep a journal as you work through the planner so you can record your ups and downs. Then, on "down" days, you can pull out the journal and reread the entries from "up" days. You'll be surprised how the small successes you record help build your faith.
- **Relationally:** This week, spend time alone with your spouse and then with the whole family.

Wake-up Call!

Most couples cite financial problems as the number-one source of marital strife.

The most important person in your life right now, if you are married, is your spouse. Let your mate know how much he or she means to you. If you have children, turn off the TV and take time to play one of their favorite games with them. If you have teenagers, just hang out with them. Make an appointment if you have to, but don't let a week go by without spending time with your family.

If you are single, don't spend all your time alone—that is a formula for depression. Call your family or take time to go out to dinner or to a movie with a friend. Commit to meet some other single people from your church this week for a fun, low-cost outing. Whatever you do, don't sit at home alone.

- **Physically:** Take time to exercise. In addition to keeping your heart strong, exercise reduces stress, helps with depression, and improves your productivity during the day. Swim, walk, jog, play basketball at the Y. Whatever sport appeals to you, commit to do it for at least thirty minutes, three times a week.
- **Mentally:** After people graduate from college, they rarely pick up a serious book. Instead, they give their minds over to cheap thrillers and romance novels—or worse, television. Try to find a good book, in addition to this one, that will help you improve some area of your life or mind, and commit to reading it for at least ten minutes a day.

At the end of each chapter in the Peace Track sections, you will find a Weekly Goals chart like the one on page 11. You can use these to keep your personal life ordered as you move toward financial health and freedom. Here is what a week's chart might look like:

Weekly Goals

	Goal	Date
Spiritual	Spend 15 minutes every morning in prayer, meditation, and planning	Start Monday, 3/3
Relational	Date night with spouse Take kids to park Saturday afternoon	Friday, 3/7 Saturday, 3/8
Physical	Run, 30 minutes	Tuesday, Thursday, Saturday
Mental	Read *FP Planner*, 10 minutes a day	1st chapter finished by 3/9

In the space provided on page 13, create an action plan for next week. Write down one spiritual, relational, physical, and mental goal and the date you intend to achieve that goal.

After you set your goals, find a "financial buddy" who can help you stick to this process. Runners testify that they run faster and better with a partner. People with friends get sick less frequently than those who spend most of their time alone. Teams frequently produce better products than individuals. Similarly, it will be easier for you to stick to the financial peace process if you adopt the financial buddy system and find someone who will encourage you to hang in there. A few guidelines for choosing a buddy are:

• Married couples: Even though your spouse is your primary support, look for another couple in similar financial circumstances with whom you can share and get feedback. Single people: Look for same-sex friends to help you as you get control of your finances.

- Commit to one contact per month with your financial buddy. This can be by phone, written note, or personal meeting.
- Make it clear that you do not expect your buddies to provide technical or mechanical financial advice. You are looking for emotional and spiritual encouragement and support. You just need them to be there for you.

Wake-up Call!

If your life is out of balance because you have an out-of-control habit, such as drinking, drugs, or gambling, what you read in this book won't help. You don't need sound financial advice. Rather, you need professional help. I am not a psychotherapist and I cannot help you overcome financial problems caused by addictions or compulsive behavior. For referrals to counselors or the appropriate help, call your local chapter of Alcoholics Anonymous.

Motivational speaker and bestselling author Zig Ziglar says a rut is a grave with both ends kicked out. Hope is the bulldozer that fills in that rut and allows you to climb out. If you embrace the principles in this book, take the baby steps, and do all the exercises in each chapter, you will get the hope to fill in your financial rut. And remember, these lessons aren't sophisticated, because financial management doesn't have to be hard to be understood or effective. I'm just giving you the same advice your grandma used to give you. The only difference: I keep my teeth in.

The Peace Track

If you are reading this book, it's likely you spend more time than you realize worrying about money. To help you get rid of energy-robbing anxiety, keep a worry log for the next week. List five fears you have about money.

1. _____
2. _____
3. _____
4. _____
5. _____

During the coming week, make a note on a separate sheet of paper, in your Day-Timer, or in a notebook every time one of those fears pops up in your mind. Then, stop yourself. Take a deep breath, and pray or take a five-minute walk. Record the results in your log. How does your thinking change after taking a break? How do you feel? Hang on to your list of fears; you'll need them again at the end of chapter 3.

Weekly Goals

	Goal	Date
Spiritual		
Relational		
Physical		
Mental		

TWO

What's a Nice Guy Like You Doing in a Place Like This?

"I'VE BEEN THINKING of declaring bankruptcy," Barry said the day he called *The Money Game*. "I just can't see how else we're going to get out of debt."

Barry and his wife, Emily, had almost $12,000 in credit card debt, a $20,000 consolidation loan, and notes on two new cars—one for $18,000 and one for $12,000. That was in addition to their $1,132 mortgage.

At age thirty-seven, Barry had been laid off three times in three years. Emily, thirty-five, worked hard as an office manager to support him and their three children—Luke, ten; Ellie, eight; and Megan, six—but her $35,000 salary just wasn't enough for a family of five to make it. So they had turned to their credit cards to pull them through the lean times.

Barry's current job paid about $35,000 a year, like Emily's, but he and Emily were still falling behind every month. Bankruptcy appealed to him because it seemed the best way to clean their slate and start over. But when I explained how it would ruin his credit for as long as ten years, it became less appealing.

"Have you thought about selling some stuff?" I asked. "You said you have two *brand-new* cars sitting in the driveway. What about selling one of those?"

"I can't sell one of our cars!" Barry exclaimed. "We have to have those. Sure, the timing wasn't great for us to go out and buy cars, but my wife and

I both work and our jobs take us to opposite sides of town. What were we supposed to do?"

In Stuff We Trust

A few weeks later, Barry and Emily enrolled in Financial Peace University. And it took more than three weeks of the seminar course to convince Barry to sell one of his new cars and replace it with a used one. That's because Barry had a classic case of stuffitis: He liked *good* stuff. He wanted to drive new cars, dress his family in designer clothes, and live in a big house. Unlike a materialist, who lives by the motto "The more, the better," how much Barry owned wasn't as important to him as the quality of stuff he owned. He wanted the *best*.

Barry's layoffs might have been the reason he and Emily were in dire financial straits, but his stuffitis magnified the problem. In fact, even if he hadn't lost his first job, the couple would still have been in serious debt because of their spending patterns.

Do you suffer from stuffitis? To find out, check the statements that follow which describe you or the way you think:

____I can't get rid of my boat/truck/Andy Warhol print. That would leave a huge hole in my life.

____It's not unusual for me to say "It's only a few dollars extra" when I'm shopping for something I want.

____I get angry when my wife/husband/friend suggests I shop for discount items. You pay for what you get, after all.

____Public school is a great idea, but my kids are going to private school, even if it means I have to cut back on our grocery spending.

____Budget, schmudget, generic brands just don't taste as good. So what's a few cents here and there?

____So I spent $100 on a pair of running shoes. The top of the line lasts longer.

If you checked more than one item above, it's likely you have a case of stuffitis. One way to keep it under control is to keep perspective on what you own.

Wearing Armani suits doesn't make you the best in the business. Driving a Jag isn't going to make you more lovable or better marriage material. "Stuff" doesn't make you special. Today's culture may attribute significance to people based on what they own and do; but our forefathers knew where true significance lay and they went so far as to announce it on our currency: "In *God* We Trust," it says—not "In *Stuff* We Trust."

Shop Therapy

Kit's troubles started during her divorce. "I had to numb the pain," she said, "so I turned to shop therapy." Friday and Saturday nights were her loneliest times because her daughters usually went out with friends or on dates. So that's when Kit chose to cloak her pain in the anonymity the mall offered.

"If I didn't have cash in the bank, I whipped out the Visa or the American Express," Kit admitted. "And if the girls asked for it, I got it. Even after the divorce, when I realized that our income had been cut off, I couldn't say no to Terri and Malinda. I could do without, but it didn't seem fair that they would have to suffer too."

When Kit's physician husband, Monroe, surprised her by serving her with divorce papers after twenty-one years of marriage, she took what she thought was the high road. During the divorce proceedings, Kit demanded that Monroe only be held responsible for supporting their two teenage daughters—Terri, nineteen, and Malinda, sixteen—until they finished college. Unfortunately, her lawyer didn't insist she protect herself financially during the divorce and get her fair share of the family savings. As a result, she barely got enough, about $800 a month, to provide for the girls, and was left with nothing for herself.

At the time, that was just fine by Kit. She had worked and put Monroe through medical school when they were first married; she figured she could put her daughters through college, if necessary, and pay for her own living expenses. The problem was she hadn't worked since the girls were born, so finding a job took longer than she anticipated. She finally found a job selling office equipment with a $28,000 base, plus commissions. But before she settled into her work, she racked up about $7,200 of credit card debt, plus a $6,500 car loan and a $600 gas bill. What's more, she bought a house with an adjustable rate mortgage that had fluctuated up and down as much as 4 percent, making her mortgage payments difficult to predict and hard to pay.

Two years after the divorce, when Kit came to FPU, she was teetering between Current and Troubled. She paid her bills on time and had clean credit. Nevertheless, buying a new set of tires would have sent her over the edge and into the Troubled category. And her shop therapy wasn't helping matters any either.

All of Kit's spending didn't ease her pain. Even after the shopping sprees, she still came home to an empty house and unbearable grief. The brightly wrapped packages, the rustle of tissue, and the thrill of new "stuff" didn't begin to fill the seemingly bottomless hole in her soul—not to mention the climbing credit card bills.

Are you using money to camouflage your feelings? Check each statement that follows which describes you or the way you think:

____ There's nothing like a trip to the mall to help relax me after an argument with my spouse or a tough week at work.

____ If you see something you like, you should buy one in each color.

____ When my ex-husband/wife buys the kids expensive presents for holidays and birthdays, I feel pressure to buy expensive presents.

____ Sometimes I feel ashamed when I come home from a shopping spree.

____ When the going gets tough, the tough go shopping.

____ I frequently hide new purchases in the closet or at the backs of drawers.

If you checked more than one of the above statements, you may have more than a bad habit.

> ### *Wake-up Call!*
>
> Studies vary, but they suggest that between 2 and 8 percent of the American population has obsessive-compulsive shopping habits. For some Americans, shopping is simply a socially acceptable painkiller that may result in a bigger-than-usual bill and a rift at home. For others, shopping too much is a disease. If you have any doubts as to which category you fall into, seek professional and/or pastoral help.

Get Rich Quick with Other People's Money

"I'm not worried about my debt anymore," Dennis told me the day we met. "I borrowed about five grand from my grandfather and invested it in a friend's T-shirt business. It's a great opportunity. He's going to set up kiosks in malls and at concerts. I could make enough money from this deal to pay off my debt and really get my new business off the ground!"

Twenty-five years old and single, Dennis graduated college with big dreams and big debt—$12,000 in credit card debt to be exact. He didn't really think anything about it, though, because as he said, "Most of my friends had even more debt than I had."

Like many college students, Dennis had fallen into the credit card trap when he started using one to pay for his books and a few other "necessities." "I was paying for most of my own school," he told me. "So I had a really tight budget. But I was also working hard as a double major and didn't want to have to take a day job while I was trying to keep my grades up. So I decided to go ahead and charge some stuff. I figured when I graduated I'd have a job lined up, and I could pay them off then."

Unfortunately, life happened to Dennis. He did get hired for a $22,000-a-year entry-level job in advertising and marketing; but after a few months, the company had to downsize and he got caught in the middle of it. "You know the rule," he told me. "Last hired, first fired. It took me six months to decide I could start my own business and make more than what someone else would pay me. But by that time I had gotten behind on all my bills, and I had people calling me. I was freaking out. I didn't want to go to my parents for help because they had always told me, 'Don't get credit cards.' Boy, were they right."

Dennis's short-term perspective, and his goal of starting his own business without any capital, made him a bankruptcy waiting to happen. Instead of building long-term security by getting out of debt and then investing wisely, he wanted immediate payoff. (For more information on safe investing, see chapter 9.) Worse, he was using someone else's money to invest in his risky venture, which put him in jeopardy of being left with a big bill if the deal went bad.

Are you vulnerable to get-rich-quick schemes and bad investments? Check each of the following statements that describes you or the way you think:

___ The only way you get ahead is by taking chances.
___ I hate to invest in something I don't understand, but the opportunity is too good to pass up.
___ I'm not sure what the product is, but the guy said it would only cost us $1,200 up front and an hour or two extra a week to sell it.
___ This property will pay for itself. Never mind that we have debt and can't afford our own house.
___ Just because you have debt doesn't mean you shouldn't invest.
___ Sometimes you have to spend a little to make a lot.

If you checked any of the above statements, then buyer beware: You may be susceptible to everything from "sophisticated" investing to pyramid schemes. Want to know the best way to get rich quick? Get rich slow. (We'll talk more about that in chapter 7.) Remember, if it sounds too good to be true, it probably is. What's more, if you have to borrow to invest—whether it's the bank's money or Great-uncle Harry's—then you are taking a risk you can't afford.

Borrowing money to build wealth isn't sophisticated; it's stupid! People lose money every day by borrowing from banks to invest in real estate or limited partnerships or stocks. Don't go there! When you spend your own cash, you take fewer chances and make better investment decisions.

The No-Manage Fund

"I'm afraid my wife operates on the 'If we have it, I spend it,' philosophy," J. G. moaned when he first came to FPU. "She never seems interested in budgeting or saving."

"I don't think I'm extravagant," Jill protested. "I just buy what we need."

In line for a promotion at the bank where he worked, J. G. currently made about $38,000. Jill, a private-school kindergarten teacher, earned $18,000. Now twenty-six, J. G. and Jill had married right out of college. But their wedded bliss was being threatened by serious financial problems and their inability to talk about them. Instead of communicating, they fought: He said she was spending too much. She said he never involved her with the finances, so how could she know where she was going wrong? Their solution was to get separate accounts, which only drove them further into their opposite corners. *Ding-ding! They're coming out fighting!*

The truth was, both J. G. and Jill had overspent, to the tune of $20,000 in credit card debt. J. G. was right; Jill had spent a lot of money on clothes and furniture. But J. G. had also accumulated a few big toys, which they were still paying off, including a $4,500 stereo system and a $1,200 road bike he bought so he could train for a triathlon. J. G. also had $6,000 in school loans they were still whittling down.

Despite their debt, J. G. and Jill tested as Currents on the financial stress test. They were never late on a bill and sometimes paid more than the minimums on their credit cards. Jill handled her money as if it were a no-manage (as opposed to a no-load) fund. Like Jill, many people just sort of live until they wake up one day and wonder, "Gosh, how did I get into debt?" (Duh.)

They don't like numbers or thinking about "all that money stuff," and in fact, they view it as sort of a pain when they're not feeling intimidated by it.

Are you a lazy money manager? Check each of the following statements that describe you or the way you think:

____Who needs a budget? I keep track of what I spend in my head.

____I intend to reconcile my bank statement every month, but something always seems to come up so that I can't get to it.

____I hate to see cash lying around: If we have it, we should either spend it or invest it in stocks.

____My spouse is the numbers person in the family. I just leave that to him/her.

____Shopping sales takes too much time, and time is money. I just go where it's convenient.

____Is a 401(k) a pair of blue jeans?

If you identify with at least one of the above, that could mean you have a devil-may-care attitude about finances, which will surely keep you teetering on the brink of financial ruin. Don't wait until you are broke to start caring about how you manage your money. Take the advice of Proverbs 6:6–11:

You lazy people can learn by watching an anthill.
Ants don't have leaders, but they store up food during harvest season.
How long will you lie there doing nothing at all? When are you going to get up and stop sleeping?
Sleep a little. Doze a little. Fold your hands and twiddle your thumbs.
Suddenly, everything is gone, as though it had been taken by an armed robber.

21

So How Do I Get Out of This Mess?

In *Seven Habits of Highly Effective People*, Dr. Stephen Covey says the number-one habit of highly effective people is that they are proactive. They "happen" to things; things don't happen to them. Throughout the rest of the book, we will address specific ways you can "happen" to your money so it doesn't control you through stuffitis, spending addictions, poor investment choices, or lack of concern. But it will take discipline and having your priorities in order to complete the work. If you're like most Americans, though, that doesn't really sound fun. In fact, it may even sound painful, because our culture is used to having everything we want *now!* We have forgotten how to delay pleasure. Instead, as motivational speaker Brian Tracy says, "We are being taught by everything around us to have *dessert before dinner."*

A dessert-first mentality will make the rest of the book hard work. It's likely that you will have to make some major lifestyle changes along the way, which may hurt a little. You may have to cut back on your spending now so you can get out of debt and save for the future. That's when it will help to have some long-term goals and priorities set. If you know what you're aiming for, you can enjoy the feeling of success when you hit it. It will also motivate you to keep going.

In the previous chapter, I mentioned an important financial principle: Money is active. Another financial principle worth remembering: *Money is amoral.* Contrary to what some people think, the Bible doesn't say "Money is the root of all evil." Rather it says, in 1 Timothy 6:10, "The *love* of money is the root of all kinds of evil." Money doesn't make you good or bad. How much you have is not a sign of your superiority or inferiority. What you do with your money, on the other hand, does reveal something about you. You can use it for good or for evil. You can spend your money on a center for underprivileged children or you can use it to build a pornography shop. You can make a lot of money and blow it on "stuff," or you can invest it for your future and give part of it away to charities.

Another person should be able to know what matters most to you by the way you live—how you spend your time and money. Take time before you proceed to part 2 of the planner to think carefully about your values and priorities. Shut your eyes and imagine someone handing you a check for a million dollars. What would you do with it? After you spend time thinking about it, write your thoughts in the space below. (The entire family can do this exercise, by the way. It will help your children learn to define their values and what's important in life.)

_____

_____

_____

_____

Write down your top five priorities. What matters most to you? Does the way you would spend your million dollars reflect those priorities?

1. _____

2. _____

3. _____

4. _____

5. _____

On a separate sheet of paper or in a notebook, keep a log for the next week of how you spend your money. At the end of the week, evaluate how your spending reflects your priorities.

There Have to Be Limits

If you plan to regain control of your finances and build wealth, you have to learn to *limit your lifestyle*. You have to look at what your income is and determine to live well below that. If you have a case of stuffitis, like most baby boomers, that's a tough task.

Experts have tracked the boomers' financial growth and spending habits for years. What they have found is that although most couples start out broke, they attempt to achieve in three to five years a lifestyle it took their parents twenty-five to thirty years to attain. And with credit, they can. Credit allows you to drive the same car as your parents, take the same vacations, eat at the same restaurants, and live only blocks away. The difference: Your parents *worked* and *saved* for years to get where they are. You *borrowed* your way into the high life—and into debt.

Taking the first baby step will force you to start examining how you spend your money and will help you begin limiting your lifestyle. So go ahead. Take baby step 1:

Put $1,000 in an emergency fund.

Here's how: Put this book down now. Hold your right hand in front of you with your elbow bent. Now reach your left hand across the back of your right wrist to where your fingertips touch your main artery. Check for a pulse.

If you are alive, you *will* experience unexpected events. To think otherwise is naive. Cars will break down when the rent is due. Wives will get pregnant when husbands are laid off. You will need to have root canal work done when your insurance has lapsed. One way you can prepare for such events is by having cash available where you can get to it easily, in a liquid account, such as a money market or savings account. That will keep you from being tempted to depend on credit cards or get-rich-quick schemes to bail you out of tough times.

One thousand dollars may sound like a lot, but you can save that much. Start by only paying the minimum on all of your bills and cutting back on all extra spending. That means no more takeout; start cooking at home. Cut back on the movies and golf matches. Then, each week place the cash you save into your emergency fund. One family built their emergency fund by saving their change at the end of each day. By the end of the year, they had almost $900 in a giant jar.

You may have only $5, $10, or $15 to set aside when you start. That's okay. The important thing is to create and implement an emergency fund action plan. Set a date—say, three months from now—and make it your goal to save $1,000 by then. Write your target date in the log on page 25. Then, list ways you can cut back, such as getting rid of the cable TV service, dropping magazine subscriptions, brown-bagging lunch instead of eating fast food. Figure out how much you can save by cutting back for the next three months. If you can't cut back enough to save $1,000, list odd jobs you can take to help save that amount. As you go along, be sure to put the money you save by cutting back into your fund. Don't spend it elsewhere.

$1,000 TARGET DATE _____

Expense to cut back   **Amount Saved**

_____   _____

_____   _____

_____   _____

_____   _____

Total   _____

Odd Jobs I Could Do   **Amount**

_____   _____

_____   _____

_____   _____

_____   _____

_____   _____

Total   _____

The Peace Track

Create your action plan for next week. Remember to write down one spiritual, relational, physical, and mental goal and the date you intend to achieve that goal.

Weekly Goals

	Goal	Date
Spiritual		
Relational		
Physical		
Mental		

Part 2

Get a Grip on Your Finances

THREE

"Budget" by Another Name— May Help

THERE'S NO WAY around it. If you want to achieve financial peace, you are going to have to budget. Even millionaires do it. When Drs. Thomas Stanley and William Danko asked American millionaires, "Do you know how much your family spends each year on food, clothing, and shelter?" two-thirds of those surveyed said yes. "Why would a millionaire need a budget?" you ask. "They became millionaires by budgeting and controlling expenses, and they maintain their affluent status that way," write Stanley and Danko in their book *The Millionaire Next Door*.

One key to managing your money well is knowing how much you have coming in and going out. Before the month begins, you need a written plan of every dollar you make and how you spend it, whether it's to save, repay debt, or have fun. That way you spend less than you make and you begin saving for the future. If you're like most people, the problem is you hate budgeting. The forms in chapters 3 and 4 will help you create an easy-to-maintain, livable budget. The hardest part of the work will be getting over any preconceived notions or fears you may have about the process. Let's examine what some of those are.

"Budget" Means Bread and Water

A derivative of the French word *bouge*, meaning a small leather purse, the word *budget* conjures notions of no money, no fun, and no way out. People tend to think you have to live a bread-and-water lifestyle when you go on a budget. On the contrary, budgets are simply meant to help you manage the flow of cash in and out of your house. In fact, if you can't get over the negative connotation of the B word, call it a cash-flow plan or a spending plan. You can still play golf on a budget; you can still go out to eat with your spouse. It doesn't matter how you spend your money as long as you do it on purpose— that is, as long as you plan to do it before the month begins.

It's a Form of Abuse

Many adults learn to hate budgets as children, when they see their parents use the plans to control each other or the kids. The budget becomes a form of abuse. "Put that down! It's not in the budget," you may have heard growing up. Maybe your parents were struggling financially. Perhaps they were taking their financial anger out on you. Whatever the reason, you learned from their nagging and negativity to hate budgeting.

Spouses also can abuse each other with budgets, particularly when they fear their mate's overspending. For example, a husband may create a budget and hand it over to his wife, expecting her to live within the means he has dictated. This can result in a major fight known as a "budget fit."

If at First You Don't Succeed, Forget It

Who hasn't tried living on a budget, only to fall off the wagon six weeks later? It happens often and for a variety of reasons. For one, you may have left out expenses, such as clothing or furniture. I have had clients tell me they can live without clothing. But as well-known financial adviser Larry Burkett says, "I've never counseled a naked couple." You have to be real! If you don't plan for the necessities—food, clothing, shelter, transportation, and utilities— then you will have to borrow money when something needs to be replaced or repaired. The result: a crashed budget.

Others overcomplicate their budget. Experts agree that it takes about two to six hours to develop an accurate plan; then, it takes less than fifteen minutes weekly to maintain it. If you are spending more time than that on your budget, either you are leaving things out, which creates a crisis every time you try to update your plan, or you have overcomplicated the plan.

"I Don't Have Time"

Frankly, you don't have the time *not* to budget. According to the Small Business Administration, the number-one reason for small-business failure: poor record keeping. When you don't take time to plan how you will spend what you earn each month, you set yourself up for debt, or worse, bankruptcy.

"I'm Afraid of What I'll Find"

"Denial ain't just a river in Egypt," says the *Saturday Night Live* character Stuart Smalley. Clients frequently tell me they don't balance their checkbooks or create cash-flow plans because they are afraid of what they'll find. They don't want to know how much they spend every month; they don't want to know how bad it really is. Others take the attitude of the late comedienne Gracie Allen: "There must be money in the bank. I still have checks!"

Wake-up Call!

You can hide your bills in a bag, but you will still owe people money. You can avoid balancing your checkbook, but that doesn't mean you have money in the bank.

It's time to quit lying to yourself and to get real about what you spend and where you spend it.

Take time to think about your feelings about budgeting. Which of the following notions describes how you think?

___ "Budget" means bread and water.
___ It's a form of abuse.
___ If at first you don't succeed, forget it.
___ "I don't have time."
___ "I'm afraid of what I'll find."

Describe the way your parents managed their finances. Did they have a budget? Who created it? How did they talk with you about finances?

_____

_____

_____

_____

What has kept you from sticking to a budget?

_____

_____

_____

When was the last time you reconciled your bank statement? What keeps you from doing this within seventy-two hours of its hitting the mailbox?

_____

_____

_____

Once you identify what's holding you back from budgeting, it's easier to move forward in the process. It also helps if you take time to determine what you are worth, or to create an equity sheet.

What Are You Worth?

Equity equals the value of what you own minus what you owe. Calculating your equity gives you a snapshot of what you are worth today. If you own a $70,000 house, for example, and you owe $20,000 on it, your equity in the house is $50,000. Next month, your home equity will increase because you will pay more of the mortgage.

For many people, filling out an equity sheet, like the one on page 35, gives them a sense of hope. In fact, some people call them "hope sheets" because they can help illustrate the progress you make in paying off your debts. Fill out one this month. Your debts may seem high and your net worth low; but in six months, when you fill out another one, you will see how far you have come: Your net worth will have increased and your debts will have decreased. An equity sheet also comes in handy if you have to sell something so you can reduce your debt because it acts as an inventory of all your valuable property.

Remember Barry and Emily, the couple who sold one of their new cars as a step to avoid bankruptcy? Their equity sheet serves as a model for you as you fill out your own. Note that they were able to determine the debt left on their house as well as on their car by calling their mortgage broker and their banker. They determined the value of their household items, jewelry, and antiques when the items were appraised for insurance. (See page 34.)

To get their total equity, Barry and Emily subtracted the total debt on the car, the credit cards and bank loan, and the house from the total value of their home, car, and the household items, jewelry, and antiques. Credit card and unsecured loans are considered negative equity.

Now, take time to fill out your own equity sheet (page 35).

When you first start budgeting, fill out an equity sheet once every six months. Then, do it every year after that. There is an additional sheet in the appendix, on page 258. Now it's time to take control of your spending by creating the budget.

Budget Step 1: What's Coming In?

The first step in creating a spending plan is determining what your income will be this month. Income sources include take-home pay, as well as money made from bonuses, rental property, royalties, freelance work, investment interest and dividends, alimony and child support, unemployment, Social Security, annuities, disability, gifts, and trust funds. It's important that you record everything you expect to receive this month, before the month begins, so you can plan how you will spend the money. (See pages 37–38.) For example, Barry and Emily's parents and grandparents send cash gifts for birthdays and

Barry and Emily's Equity Sheet

ITEM/Describe	Value	−	Debt	=	Equity
Real Estate _____House_____	$120,000	−	$ 95,000	=	$ 25,000
Real Estate _____		−		=	
Car _____2-year-old Camry_____	$ 18,000	−	$ 11,000	=	$ 7,000
Car _____Used_____	$ 2,500	−	0	=	$ 2,500
Cash on Hand	$ 300	−	0	=	$ 300
Checking Account 1	$ 3,000	−	0	=	$ 3,000
Checking Account 2		−		=	
Savings Account 1		−		=	
Savings Account 2		−		=	
Money Market Account	$ 1,000	−	0	=	$ 1,000
Mutual Funds		−		=	
Retirement Plan	$ 4,500	−	0	=	$ 4,500
Stocks or Bonds		−		=	
Cash Value Insurance		−		=	
Household Items	$ 10,000	−	0	=	$ 10,000
Jewelry	$ 3,500	−	0	=	$ 3,500
Antiques	$ 5,000	−	0	=	$ 5,000
Boat		−		=	
Unsecured Debt (Negative)		−	$ 20,000	=	$−20,000
Credit Card Debt (Negative)		−	$ 11,665	=	$−11,665
Other _____		−		=	
Other _____		−		=	
Other _____		−		=	
TOTAL	$167,800	−	$137,665	=	$ 30,135

Your Equity Sheet

ITEM/Describe	Value	–	Debt	=	Equity
Real Estate _____	_____	–	_____	=	_____
Real Estate _____	_____	–	_____	=	_____
Car _____	_____	–	_____	=	_____
Car _____	_____	–	_____	=	_____
Cash on Hand	_____	–	_____	=	_____
Checking Account 1	_____	–	_____	=	_____
Checking Account 2	_____	–	_____	=	_____
Savings Account 1	_____	–	_____	=	_____
Savings Account 2	_____	–	_____	=	_____
Money Market Account	_____	–	_____	=	_____
Mutual Funds	_____	–	_____	=	_____
Retirement Plan	_____	–	_____	=	_____
Stocks or Bonds	_____	–	_____	=	_____
Cash Value Insurance	_____	–	_____	=	_____
Household Items	_____	–	_____	=	_____
Jewelry	_____	–	_____	=	_____
Antiques	_____	–	_____	=	_____
Boat	_____	–	_____	=	_____
Unsecured Debt (Negative)	_____	–	_____	=	_____
Credit Card Debt (Negative)	_____	–	_____	=	_____
Other _____	_____	–	_____	=	_____
Other _____	_____	–	_____	=	_____
Other _____	_____	–	_____	=	_____
TOTAL	_____	–	_____	=	_____

anniversaries throughout the year. On the months they expect to receive, say, a $100 check, they write that amount on the "Cash Gifts" line. That way they will spend that $100 on purpose when they receive it instead of get the check in the mail and think, Whoa! Extra money! Party on dude! Most of us blow money if we don't plan how to spend it first.

This month, Barry and Emily aren't expecting any cash gifts. They will only receive their monthly salary, so their income source sheet looks pretty bare—something a lot of us can relate to.

Barry and Emily's Income Sources

Source	Amount	Period/Describe
Salary 1	$2,316	Emily's monthly take-home pay
Salary 2	$2,433	Barry's monthly take-home pay
Salary 3		
Bonus		
Self-employment		
Interest Income		
Dividend Income		
Royalty Income		
Rents		
Notes		
Alimony		
Child Support		
AFDC		
Unemployment		
Social Security		
Pension		
Annuity		
Disability Income		
Cash Gifts		
Trust Fund		
Other		

Continued on next page

Other	_____	_____
Other	_____	_____
TOTAL	_____	_____

Note that Barry and Emily's salaries are reported in terms of what they will actually bring home this month. To figure this out, look at the net pay amount on your last pay stub. That is your take-home pay for that pay period. If you are paid weekly, multiply that amount by four. If you are paid biweekly, multiply by two. If you have an irregular income because you are a freelancer or work for sales commissions, you should estimate this month's take-home pay based on what you made last year or on the contracts you have signed for the year; then, record the amount on the "Self-employment" line. Stay conservative in your estimations.

Now, fill out your own income source sheet.

Your Income Sources

Source	Amount	Period/Describe
Salary 1	_____	_____
Salary 2	_____	_____
Salary 3	_____	_____
Bonus	_____	_____
Self-employment	_____	_____
Interest Income	_____	_____
Dividend Income	_____	_____
Royalty Income	_____	_____
Rents	_____	_____
Notes	_____	_____
Alimony	_____	_____
Child Support	_____	_____
AFDC	_____	_____
Unemployment	_____	_____
Social Security	_____	_____

Continued on next page

Source	Amount	Period/Describe
Pension	_____	_____
Annuity	_____	_____
Disability Income	_____	_____
Cash Gifts	_____	_____
Trust Fund	_____	_____
Other	_____	_____
Other	_____	_____
Other	_____	_____
TOTAL	_____	_____

Before every month begins, you need to review your income source sheet and update it. Salaries change; bonuses come in. One month you may receive a dividend or royalty income. There is an additional income source sheet in the appendix, page 259, for you to use when you update your budget next month. For now, hold on to this income source sheet; you'll need it when you create your monthly cash-flow plan, on page 48.

Budget Step 2: What Income Goes Out?

Now we come to the tricky part of budgeting: planning how you will spend your money. It's easy to leave out or underestimate your expenses. Quarterly or semiannual payments, such as health insurance, medical bills, real estate taxes, and insurance premiums, can sneak up on you and wreak havoc on your budget if you don't plan and save for them each month. Other expenses, such as school supplies or organization dues, may seem so insignificant you fail to include them in your budget. Then when you have to pay for them, you don't have the money.

The best way to make sure you don't overlook any monthly expenses when creating your budget is to convert large expenses into monthly payments and then categorize them, along with the smaller expenses.

You will have to estimate some of the expenses on your monthly breakdown of expenses list (see page 41). For example, you can figure out what you will spend on medical bills for the rest of the year by looking through last year's checkbook and determining how much you spent on basic health and wellness—annual checkups, semiannual dental visits, anything not covered by your insurance. The same goes for clothing, tuition, vacations, gifts, and home repairs.

It may be tempting to skip the "Replace Furniture" and "Replace Car" categories if you have just bought new furniture or a new car, but don't. Even if your new furniture will last a lifetime, it's likely you will still want new carpet, new draperies, a reupholstered sofa after the kids grow up, or even a few collectibles from time to time.

Barry and Emily's monthly expenses breakdown appears on page 40. Note that Barry and Emily are not saving for a new-car category. This is because they did not pay cash for Emily's car and they now have a car payment. (They did sell Barry's new car and replaced it with a $2,500 clunker.) With all of their other expenses, they can't afford to save for the next car, which is going to make it harder on them later. Under the "Banknote" category, they simply wrote the monthly amount because they know what their monthly payment is.

Now, complete your own monthly breakdown of expenses on page 41.

Be sure you save the monthly amounts until the bills are due. This way you can avoid scrambling around, looking for the extra cash to pay the bills on the month they need to be paid.

After you convert large expenses into monthly payments, you can use the cash-flow plan, or budget, to categorize them and your smaller expenses. The major categories in the Financial Peace budget include charitable gifts, savings, housing, utilities, food, transportation, clothing, medical/health, personal, blow, recreation, and debts. The "Blow" category is money you can spend however you want. Some people call it mad money; others call it fun money; I call it blow money, in memory of my former budget system—if I had it, I blew it.

Record your monthly breakdown of expenses payments in the monthly cash-flow plan on page 48. Then fill in what you think you will need for the other expenses. If you have any questions about how much you should budget

Barry and Emily's Monthly Breakdown of Expenses

Item Needed	Annual Amount	÷ 12 =	Monthly Amount
Real Estate Taxes		÷ 12 =	
Homeowners Insurance	$ 720	÷ 12 =	$ 60
Home Repairs	$1,200	÷ 12 =	$100
Replace Furniture	$ 600	÷ 12 =	$ 50
Medical Bills	$1,500	÷ 12 =	$125
Health Insurance	$3,600	÷ 12 =	$300
Life Insurance	$ 840	÷ 12 =	$ 70
Disability Insurance		÷ 12 =	
Car Insurance	$1,200	÷ 12 =	$100
Car Repair	$1,000	÷ 12 =	$ 83
License/Tags	$ 120	÷ 12 =	$ 10
Replace Car		÷ 12 =	
Clothing: Adult	$1,800	÷ 12 =	$150
Clothing: Children	$ 900	÷ 12 =	$ 75
Tuition		÷ 12 =	
Banknotes		÷ 12 =	$850
IRS		÷ 12 =	
Vacation	$1,200	÷ 12 =	$100
Gifts (Including Christmas)	$1,500	÷ 12 =	$125
Other (Giving)	$5,700	÷ 12 =	$475

for an item, look through your checkbook for the past three months. On a separate sheet of paper, record what you spent for that item each of the three months; then, take the average amount and use that as your estimate of what you will spend this month. Hint: The first few months you budget, pad necessities, such as food and gasoline. Budget more than you think you will need because you always spend more than you think you do.

Add the items within each category to get the category subtotal. Then figure out the grand total of your monthly expenses by tallying the category

Your Monthly Breakdown of Expenses

Item Needed	Annual Amount	÷ 12 =	Monthly Amount
Real Estate Taxes		÷ 12 =	
Homeowners Insurance		÷ 12 =	
Home Repairs		÷ 12 =	
Replace Furniture		÷ 12 =	
Medical Bills		÷ 12 =	
Health Insurance		÷ 12 =	
Life Insurance		÷ 12 =	
Disability Insurance		÷ 12 =	
Car Insurance		÷ 12 =	
Car Repair		÷ 12 =	
License/Tags		÷ 12 =	
Replace Car		÷ 12 =	
Clothing: Adult		÷ 12 =	
Clothing: Children		÷ 12 =	
Tuition		÷ 12 =	
Banknotes		÷ 12 =	
IRS		÷ 12 =	
Vacation		÷ 12 =	
Gifts (Include Christmas)		÷ 12 =	
Other		÷ 12 =	

subtotals. Finally, subtract this month's income (see page 38) from the grand total. The balance must be zero. If it isn't, then redo the budget until it equals zero. (It's a good idea to use a pencil when you're creating your first budget.)

Keep in mind that your budget is for *this* month. You are not going to create one generic budget because your expenses and even your income may change from month to month. (You hope your expenses will decrease.)

Here's what Barry and Emily's first plan looked like:

Barry and Emily's Monthly Cash-Flow Plan

Category	Budgeted $	Subtotal
Charitable Gifts	$ 475	
		$ 475
Savings		
Emergency Fund	$ 50	
Retirement Fund		
College Fund		
		$ 50
Housing		
First Mortgage	$1,132	
Second Mortgage		
Real Estate Taxes		
Homeowners Insurance	$ 60	
Home Repairs	$ 100	
Replace Furniture	$ 50	
Other _____		
		$1,342
Utilities		
Electricity	$ 70	
Water	$ 35	
Gas	$ 60	
Phone	$ 80	
Trash		
Cable	$ 25	
Computer On-line	$ 20	
		$ 290
Food		
Grocery	$ 600	
Restaurants	$ 100	
		$ 700

Category	Budgeted $	Subtotal
Transportation		
Car Payment 1	$ 335	
Car Payment 2		
Gas and Oil	$ 90	
Repairs and Tires	$ 83	
Car Insurance	$ 100	
License and Taxes	$ 10	
Car Replacement		
		$ 618
Clothing		
Children	$ 75	
Adults	$ 150	
Cleaning/Laundry	$ 65	
		$ 290
Medical/Health		
Disability Insurance		
Health Insurance	$ 300	
Doctor Bills	$ 80	
Dentist	$ 45	
Optometrist		
Drugs	$ 10	
Other _____		
		$ 435
Personal		
Life Insurance	$ 70	
Child Care		
Baby-sitter	$ 40	
Toiletries	$ 50	
Cosmetics	$ 20	
Hair Care	$ 50	

Continued on next page

Category	Budgeted $	Subtotal
Personal (*cont.*)		
Education/Adult		
School Tuition		
School Supplies	$100	
Child Support		
Alimony		
Subscriptions		
Organization Dues	$ 25	
Gifts (Christmas)	$125	
Miscellaneous		
		$ 480
Blow$$	$100	
		$ 100
Recreation		
Entertainment	$100	
Vacation	$100	
		$ 200
Debts ($0, you hope)		
Visa 1	$ 24	
Visa 2	$ 10	
MasterCard 1	$ 10	
MasterCard 2	$148	
American Express		
Discover Card		
Gas Card 1	$ 83	
Gas Card 2		
Dept. Store Card 1	$120	
Dept. Store Card 2		
Finance Company 1		
Finance Company 2		
Credit Line		
Student Loan 1		

Category	Budgeted $	Subtotal
Debts (*cont.*)		
Student Loan 2	_____	
Other <u>Bank Loan</u>	$567	
Other _____	_____	
Other _____	_____	
		$ 962
GRAND TOTAL		$5,942
–TOTAL INCOME		$4,750
ZERO		$1,192

Wake-up Call!

A negative balance means you have to cut back and/or find ways to earn more.

"Twelve hundred dollars in the red!" Barry exclaimed when he and Emily completed their budget.

"What are we going to do?" Emily asked.

People often discover they have been spending more than they make when they finally sit down to create a budget. If you, like Emily and Barry, are in that predicament, don't panic. Instead, take a deep breath, calm yourself, and start looking for where you can cut back.

It wasn't too hard for Barry and Emily to figure out how they were going in the hole: They carried $962 a month in credit card debt and bank payments. (Except for the gas and department store credit card, the payments under "Debt" are their monthly minimums.) Even if they had had no debt, however, they would still have been overspending (or underearning) around $230. So they decided to revise their budget. To help them decide where to reduce their spending, they used the "Recommended Percentage of Household Income" chart that follows.

Recommended Percentage of Household Income

Charitable Gifts	10–15%
Savings	10–15%
Housing	25–35%
Utilities (electric, water, gas, and phone)	5–10%
Food	5–15%
Transportation	10–15%
Clothing	2–7%
Medical/Health	5–10%
Personal	5–10%
Recreation	5–10%
Blow	2–5%
Debts	5–10%

Barry and Emily compared the percentage of household income they were spending on the major categories in their budget with the chart's recommended percentages. Then, they created their own chart, below, which reflects their findings:

Barry and Emily's Percentage of Household Income

Charitable Gifts	10%
Savings	1%
Housing	28%
Utilities	6%
Food	15%
Transportation	13%
Clothing	6%
Medical/Health	9%
Personal	10%
Recreation	4%
Blow	2%
Debts	20%

The couple quickly determined that the only category where they were overpaying was "Debts." They also noted that they were shortchanging themselves on saving and recreation and agreed to pump those up later, after they paid off their debt. For now, they needed to stop the bleeding in their wallets.

"Help! My Budget Has Fallen and It Can't Get Up!"

When you find yourself with too much month at the end of the money, take these steps:

- Sell something to help reduce debt. Get radical. Sell so much stuff the kids are afraid they are the next on the auction block.
- Cut back on your spending.
- Look for extra work.

Barry and Emily pumped the life back into their budget by deciding to sell something. They looked back at their equity sheet and found an antique they could sell for $1,500. Then they used that money to pay off the $83 balance on the gas card, the $120 department store balance, the $700 Visa 2 balance, and the $597 MasterCard balance. As a result, they were able to eliminate $223 in monthly expenses (their minimum payments on the Visa and the MasterCard were $10 each).

Barry and Emily then attacked the budget, trimming expenses. They didn't want to cut back on giving to their local church. So they found other places they could temporarily cut back for a savings of $545 a month. The items they cut included:

Home repairs and furniture	$150
Cut out cable and Internet access	$45
Cut back on groceries and eating out	$150
Blow money	$100
Vacation	$100
Total	**$545**

Barry and Emily weren't giving up the possibility of ever going on a vacation or having new furniture. But they did agree they could shop smarter and find cheaper ways to have fun until they could get back on their feet financially. Cutting back wasn't the only solution, however.

The couple needed to earn an extra $424 a month in order to break even. So Barry decided to look for part-time work in addition to his current employment. What he found was a job delivering newspapers, which paid $600 a month after taxes. Not only did that help Barry and Emily break even, but it gave them an additional $176 to put toward retiring their credit card debt.

We will talk more specifically about how to get out of debt in chapter 5, but for now, you can see what you need to do to devise a zero-balance budget. Note that the percentage of take-home pay is included as one of the columns in your monthly cash-flow plan below, and filling in these percentages will quickly show you if your plan is out of balance. Now, fill out your own monthly cash-flow plan. (There is an additional copy of the cash-flow plan in the appendix, on page 260.)

Your Monthly Cash-Flow Plan

Category	Budgeted $	Subtotal	% Take-Home Pay
Charitable Gifts	_____		
		_____	_____
SAVINGS			
Emergency Fund	_____		
Retirement Fund	_____		
College Fund	_____		
		_____	_____
HOUSING			
First Mortgage	_____		
Second Mortgage	_____		
Real Estate Taxes	_____		
Homeowners Insurance	_____		
Home Repairs	_____		

Continued on next page

Category	Budgeted $	Subtotal	% Take-Home Pay
HOUSING (*cont.*)			
Replace Furniture	_____		
Other _____	_____		
		_____	_____
UTILITIES			
Electricity	_____		
Water	_____		
Gas	_____		
Phone	_____		
Trash	_____		
Cable	_____		
Computer On-line	_____		
		_____	_____
FOOD			
Grocery	_____		
Restaurants	_____		
		_____	_____
TRANSPORTATION			
Car Payment	_____		
Car Payment	_____		
Gas and Oil	_____		
Repairs and Tires	_____		
Car Insurance	_____		
License and Taxes	_____		
Car Replacement	_____		
CLOTHING		_____	_____
Children	_____		
Adults	_____		
Cleaning/Laundry	_____		
		_____	_____

Continued on next page

Category	Budgeted $	Subtotal	% Take-Home Pay
MEDICAL/HEALTH			
Disability Insurance	_____		
Health Insurance	_____		
Doctor Bills	_____		
Dentist	_____		
Optometrist	_____		
Drugs	_____		
Other _____	_____		
		_____	_____
PERSONAL			
Life Insurance	_____		
Child Care	_____		
Baby-sitter	_____		
Toiletries	_____		
Cosmetics	_____		
Hair Care	_____		
Education/Adult	_____		
School Tuition	_____		
School Supplies	_____		
Child Support	_____		
Alimony	_____		
Subscriptions	_____		
Organization Dues	_____		
Gifts (Christmas)	_____		
Miscellaneous	_____		
BLOW $$	_____	_____	_____
RECREATION		_____	_____
Entertainment	_____		
Vacation	_____		
		_____	_____

Continued on next page

Category	Budgeted $	Subtotal	% Take-Home Pay
DEBTS ($0, you hope)			
Visa 1	_____		
Visa 2	_____		
MasterCard 1	_____		
MasterCard 2	_____		
American Express	_____		
Discover Card	_____		
Gas Card 1	_____		
Gas Card 2	_____		
Dept. Store Card 1	_____		
Dept. Store Card 2	_____		
Finance Company 1	_____		
Finance Company 2	_____		
Credit Line	_____		
Student Loan 1	_____		
Student Loan 2	_____		
Other _____	_____		
Other _____	_____		
Other _____	_____		
		_____	_____
GRAND TOTAL		_____	
−TOTAL INCOME		_____	
		_____	

If, like Barry and Emily, you come up with a negative balance, you have some more work to do. Look at your percentages and see where you can cut back. Refer to your equity sheet to see whether there is something you can sell. Consider taking a second job. It may take a while to come up with a solution, but don't put off resolving the issue, bringing your balance to zero. Complete your budget today!

There is a chance, of course, that your budget will have a positive balance.

One client, for example, had $1,200 left over at the end of his plan! If you have money left over at the bottom of the budget, find a category in the plan where you can spend it, save it, give it, or blow it. Review your expenses and make sure you have been realistic about how much you need to spend. Have you sufficiently budgeted for every subcategory? If so, then plan to increase your charitable giving and your saving. Whatever you do, though, plan how you will use that money *before* the month begins. Spend, save, give, or blow your money *on purpose.* Don't let the money go unaccounted for.

Budget Step 3: Give Every Dollar a Name

The final step of budgeting helps you give every dollar you earn a name so you'll know exactly where it goes. You will never again have to wonder how you got into debt or why you can't seem to save because you will have written the answer on the allocated spending plan. (If you earn an irregular income, use the irregular income plan on page 63.) Here's how it works.

There are four columns representing the four potential income periods of the month. This system assumes that you are being paid on a weekly basis; even if this is not the case, fill in the dates of the four pay periods in the month. Then, fill in the income you receive for each period. Emily and Barry get paid twice a month, but on different days. Barry also gets paid $150 a week for the newspaper delivery. Two-income couples should add their incomes on the days they both receive money. Remember to include all your income, not just the salary you earn.

Then, begin to allot a portion of each check or dividend you receive to the various expenses you need to pay during that period. Some expenses will be paid every pay period; others will be paid only once or twice a month. Start with the total amount you have to spend in each pay period; as you fill in an expense, deduct it from the money available for that pay period. You will write the new total to be spent to the right of the expense (after the slash provided). Here is Barry and Emily's spending plan:

Barry and Emily's Allocated Spending Plan

Income Period	3/7	3/14	3/21	3/28
Income	$1,308	$1,367	$1,308	$1,367
Item				
CHARITABLE GIFTS	$119/$1,189	$119/$1,248	$119/$1,189	$118/$1,249
SAVINGS				
Emergency Fund	$50/$1,139	/	/	/
Retirement Fund	/	/	/	/
College Fund	/	/	/	/
HOUSING				
First Mortgage	/	$1,132/$116	/	/
Second Mortgage	/	/	/	/
Real Estate Taxes	/	/	/	/
Homeowners Ins.	/	$60/$56	/	/
Home Repairs	/	/	/	/
Replace Furniture	/	/	/	/
Other _____	/	/	/	/
UTILITIES				
Electricity	/	/	$70/$1,119	/
Water	/	$35/$21	/	/
Gas	/	/	$60/$1,059	/
Phone	/	/	$80/$979	/

Continued on next page

UTILITIES (*cont.*)

Trash	/	/	/	/
Cable	/	/	/	/
Computer On-line	/	/	/	/

FOOD

Grocery	$250/$889	/	$250/$729	/
Restaurants	/	/	/	$50/$1,199

TRANSPORTATION

Car Payment	$335/$554	/	/	/
Car Payment	/	/	/	/
Gas and Oil	$46/$508	/	$44/$685	/
Repairs and Tires	$41/$467	/	/	$42/$1,157
Car Insurance	/	/	$100/$585	/
License and Taxes	/	/	$10/$575	/
Car Replacement	/	/	/	/

CLOTHING

Children	/	/	/	$75/$1,082
Adults	/	/	/	$150/$932
Cleaning/Laundry	/	/	/	$65/$867

MEDICAL/HEALTH

Disability Insurance	/	/	/	/
Health Insurance	/	/	/	$300/$567

MEDICAL/HEALTH (*cont.*)

Doctor	/	/	/	$80/$487
Dentist	/	/	/	$45/$442
Optometrist	/	/	/	/
Drugs	/	/	/	$10/$432

PERSONAL

Life Insurance	$70/$397	/	/	/
Child Care	/	/	/	/
Baby-sitter	$20/$377	/	/	$20/$412
Toiletries	/	/	/	$50/$362
Cosmetics	/	/	/	$20/$342
Hair Care	/	/	/	$50/$292
Education/Adult	/	/	/	/
School Tuition	/	/	/	/
School Supplies	$100/$277	/	/	/
Child Support	/	/	/	/
Alimony	/	/	/	/
Subscriptions	/	/	/	/
Organization Dues	$25/$252	/	/	/
Gifts	$25/$227	$21/0	/	$79/$213
Miscellaneous	/	/	/	/
BLOW $$	/	/	/	/

Continued on next page

RECREATION

Entertainment	$79/$148	/	$8/$567	$13/$200
Vacation	/	/	/	/

DEBTS ($0, YOU HOPE)

Visa 1	/	/	/	$24/$176
Visa 2	/	/	/	/
MasterCard 1	/	/	/	/
MasterCard 2	$148/0	/	/	$176/0
American Express	/	/	/	/
Discover Card	/	/	/	/
Gas Card 1	/	/	/	/
Gas Card 2	/	/	/	/
Dept. Store Card 1	/	/	/	/
Dept. Store Card 2	/	/	/	/
Finance Company 1	/	/	/	/
Finance Company 2	/	/	/	/
Credit Line	/	/	/	/
Student Loan 1	/	/	/	/
Student Loan 2	/	/	/	/
Other Debt _____	/	/	$567/0	/
Other _____	/	/	/	/
Other _____	/	/	/	/

Note that Barry happened to make $185 extra this month, which he used to reduce his credit card debt. He and Emily also cashed a check for two weeks' worth of gas and groceries at a time and carried cash with them instead of relying on credit cards. They were starting to realize that the only way to get out of debt is to quit spending and borrowing.

Take time now to complete the allocated spending plan. If you are self-employed or work on commission or royalties, you won't be able to complete the allocated spending plan because of your unpredictable income. Instead, skip to the irregular income plan on page 61.

Your Allocated Spending Plan

Income Period	/	/	/	/
Income				
Item				
CHARITABLE GIFTS	/	/	/	/
SAVINGS				
Emergency Fund	/	/	/	/
Retirement Fund	/	/	/	/
College Fund	/	/	/	/
HOUSING				
First Mortgage	/	/	/	/
Second Mortgage	/	/	/	/
Real Estate Taxes	/	/	/	/
Homeowners Ins.	/	/	/	/
Home Repairs	/	/	/	/

Continued on next page

HOUSING (*cont.*)

Replace Furniture _____ / _____ _____ / _____ _____ / _____ _____ / _____

Other _____ _____ / _____ _____ / _____ _____ / _____ _____ / _____

UTILITIES

Electricity _____ / _____ _____ / _____ _____ / _____ _____ / _____

Water _____ / _____ _____ / _____ _____ / _____ _____ / _____

Gas _____ / _____ _____ / _____ _____ / _____ _____ / _____

Phone _____ / _____ _____ / _____ _____ / _____ _____ / _____

Trash _____ / _____ _____ / _____ _____ / _____ _____ / _____

Cable _____ / _____ _____ / _____ _____ / _____ _____ / _____

Computer On-line _____ / _____ _____ / _____ _____ / _____ _____ / _____

FOOD

Grocery _____ / _____ _____ / _____ _____ / _____ _____ / _____

Restaurants _____ / _____ _____ / _____ _____ / _____ _____ / _____

TRANSPORTATION

Car Payment _____ / _____ _____ / _____ _____ / _____ _____ / _____

Car Payment _____ / _____ _____ / _____ _____ / _____ _____ / _____

Gas and Oil _____ / _____ _____ / _____ _____ / _____ _____ / _____

Repair and Tires _____ / _____ _____ / _____ _____ / _____ _____ / _____

Car Insurance _____ / _____ _____ / _____ _____ / _____ _____ / _____

License and Taxes _____ / _____ _____ / _____ _____ / _____ _____ / _____

Car Replacement _____ / _____ _____ / _____ _____ / _____ _____ / _____

CLOTHING

Children   _____/_____   _____/_____   _____/_____   _____/_____

Adults   _____/_____   _____/_____   _____/_____   _____/_____

Cleaning/Laundry   _____/_____   _____/_____   _____/_____   _____/_____

MEDICAL/HEALTH

Disability Insurance   _____/_____   _____/_____   _____/_____   _____/_____

Health Insurance   _____/_____   _____/_____   _____/_____   _____/_____

Doctor   _____/_____   _____/_____   _____/_____   _____/_____

Dentist   _____/_____   _____/_____   _____/_____   _____/_____

Optometrist   _____/_____   _____/_____   _____/_____   _____/_____

Drugs   _____/_____   _____/_____   _____/_____   _____/_____

PERSONAL

Life Insurance   _____/_____   _____/_____   _____/_____   _____/_____

Child Care   _____/_____   _____/_____   _____/_____   _____/_____

Baby-sitter   _____/_____   _____/_____   _____/_____   _____/_____

Toiletries   _____/_____   _____/_____   _____/_____   _____/_____

Cosmetics   _____/_____   _____/_____   _____/_____   _____/_____

Hair Care   _____/_____   _____/_____   _____/_____   _____/_____

Education/Adult   _____/_____   _____/_____   _____/_____   _____/_____

School Tuition   _____/_____   _____/_____   _____/_____   _____/_____

School Supplies   _____/_____   _____/_____   _____/_____   _____/_____

Child Support   _____/_____   _____/_____   _____/_____   _____/_____

Continued on next page

PERSONAL (*cont.*)

Alimony _____ / _____   _____ / _____   _____ / _____   _____ / _____

Subscriptions _____ / _____   _____ / _____   _____ / _____   _____ / _____

Organization Dues _____ / _____   _____ / _____   _____ / _____   _____ / _____

Gifts (inc. Christmas) _____ / _____   _____ / _____   _____ / _____   _____ / _____

Miscellaneous _____ / _____   _____ / _____   _____ / _____   _____ / _____

BLOW $$ _____ / _____   _____ / _____   _____ / _____   _____ / _____

RECREATION

Entertainment _____ / _____   _____ / _____   _____ / _____   _____ / _____

Vacation _____ / _____   _____ / _____   _____ / _____   _____ / _____

DEBTS ($0, YOU HOPE)

Visa 1 _____ / _____   _____ / _____   _____ / _____   _____ / _____

Visa 2 _____ / _____   _____ / _____   _____ / _____   _____ / _____

MasterCard 1 _____ / _____   _____ / _____   _____ / _____   _____ / _____

MasterCard 2 _____ / _____   _____ / _____   _____ / _____   _____ / _____

American Express _____ / _____   _____ / _____   _____ / _____   _____ / _____

Discover Card _____ / _____   _____ / _____   _____ / _____   _____ / _____

Gas Card 1 _____ / _____   _____ / _____   _____ / _____   _____ / _____

Gas Card 2 _____ / _____   _____ / _____   _____ / _____   _____ / _____

Dept. Store Card 1 _____ / _____   _____ / _____   _____ / _____   _____ / _____

Dept. Store Card 2 _____ / _____   _____ / _____   _____ / _____   _____ / _____

Finance Company 1 _____ / _____   _____ / _____   _____ / _____   _____ / _____

DEBTS *(cont.)*

Finance Company 2	___ / ___	___ / ___	___ / ___	___ / ___
Credit Line	___ / ___	___ / ___	___ / ___	___ / ___
Student Loan 1	___ / ___	___ / ___	___ / ___	___ / ___
Student Loan 2	___ / ___	___ / ___	___ / ___	___ / ___
Other _____	___ / ___	___ / ___	___ / ___	___ / ___
Other _____	___ / ___	___ / ___	___ / ___	___ / ___
Other _____	___ / ___	___ / ___	___ / ___	___ / ___

Irregular Income

The irregular income plan helps you plan your expenses when you earn non-monthly commissions or royalties. Here's how it works: Look at the categories from your monthly cash-flow plan and ask yourself, "If I only have enough money this month to cover one expense, what will that be?" Then list the expense in the first blank under "Item," and fill in the amount. Continue listing your payments in order of importance. As you go, add each line to the one before it to get the cumulative amount, and continue the list until you are well past what you are likely to earn. Then, when you get a check, see how far down the list you can go.

Kit's top priority was to pay her mortgage, so she wrote that in the first blank. She also received a monthly income of $1,983 plus $1,000 in child support. Every quarter, she received between a $1,500 and $1,750 bonus. On those months, she planned to increase her debt payments, as well as save extra for the retirement and college fund, her emergency fund, and large expenses, such as insurance and taxes. Here's how Kit's irregular income plan looked the month she received her bonus:

Kit's Irregular Income Plan

Item	Amount	Cumulative Amount
Giving	$300	$ 300
Emergency Fund	$300	$ 600
Retirement Fund	$300	$ 900
College Fund	$150	$1,050
Mortgage	$640	$1,690
Homeowners Insurance	$ 50	$1,740
Electricity	$ 80	$1,820
Water	$ 35	$1,855
Gas	$ 40	$1,895
Phone	$ 50	$1,945
Trash	$ 30	$1,975
Groceries	$400	$2,375
Car Payment	$270	$2,645
Gas/Oil	$ 80	$2,725
Car Insurance	$ 50	$2,775
Clothing	$150	$2,925
Health Insurance	$300	$3,225
Doctor Bills	$100	$3,325
Dentist	$ 50	$3,375

Item	Amount	Cumulative Amount
Optometrist	$ 17	$3,392
School Supplies (includes ball games, etc.)	$ 50	$3,442
Visa	$300	$3,742
MasterCard	$300	$4,042
Furniture	$375	$4,417
Toiletries	$ 50	$4,467
Cosmetics	$ 25	$4,492
Hair Care	$ 60	$4,552
Cable	$ 25	$4,577
Gifts	$125	$4,702
Blow	$100	$4,802
Vacation	$ 91	$4,893

Using Kit as a model, complete your own irregular income plan. If you find that you are projecting that you will spend more than you make, go back and look at how Barry and Emily lowered their spending on page 47. Beware: Urgent expenses have a way of taking priority over important expenses, such as the emergency fund.

Your Irregular Income Plan

Item	Amount	Cumulative Amount

Continued on next page

Item	Amount	Cumulative Amount

Item	Amount	Cumulative Amount
_____	_____	_____
_____	_____	_____
_____	_____	_____
_____	_____	_____
_____	_____	_____
_____	_____	_____

So Now What?

It's time to put your plan into action. For the next ninety days, commit to live by your budget. That's less than 1 percent of your life—not much time to spend on a plan that can change your financial life forever. In the next chapter, you will be asked to record what you actually spend during the month and compare it to the budget you have created. Then you will have a chance to fine-tune your plan.

The Peace Track

Baby Step Checkup

How far have you come taking baby step 1? Check "Done" if you have completed it. If you are still working on saving that $1,000, think of ways you can move toward that goal and record them in the column "Action Needed to Complete." Then give yourself a date to complete the step.

Baby Step	Done	Action Needed to Complete	Date
1. Save $1,000 in an emergency fund.			

In chapter 1, you wrote a list of five fears you have about money and kept a log of every time the fear popped up during the week. Take time this week to pull out your list (page 13), along with the log you kept that week, and look them over. Record below how many of those fears have become reality.

_____

_____

If you left a blank space above, it's not surprising. Dale Carnegie said that 80 percent of what we worry about never happens. Don't most of your worries seem small now that some time has passed? The farther you move down the road to financial peace, the farther away from your financial worries you will get. You will gain more perspective on—and control over—your finances, and your fears will gradually cease.

Use the space provided to create an action plan for next week.

Weekly Goals

	Goal	Date
Spiritual		
Relational		
Physical		
Mental		

Beat Budget Blunders

THE HARDEST PART of budgeting is sticking to it. Everywhere you turn, it seems there are traps you can fall into that make it almost impossible to live by your budget. Reading and doing the exercises in this chapter can help, but it will take work. Starting in this chapter, you are going to live on the envelope system, a time-honored method of cash management, *and* record what you actually spend.

Before you launch into any of the exercises, read the entire chapter. Then, come back and start filling out the budget form on page 74. You can use Barry and Emily's monthly cash-flow plan (below) as an example. Note that in the first column they recorded what they originally budgeted on page 42, taking into account the cuts they made. They also added the $600 Barry was bringing home from his newspaper delivery job to the "Total Income." Then they recorded what they actually spent throughout the month in the far right column.

Note that Barry and Emily's "Amount Spent" column didn't match their "Budgeted" column. They didn't visit the dentist this month, so they saved the $45 they had budgeted for that in their emergency fund. They were also able to pay $176 extra on their Visa bill. Unfortunately, they overspent in two areas: groceries, by $100, and eating out, by $50.

"It's true," Barry confirmed when we talked about it at FPU. "Some friends invited us out to dinner this weekend, and we wound up going to this exclusive

Barry and Emily's Monthly Cash-Flow Plan

Category	Budgeted	Subtotal	% Take-Home	Amount Spent
Charitable Gifts	$ 475			$ 475
		$ 475	9%	$ 475
Savings				
Emergency Fund	$ 50			$ 95
Retirement Fund				
College Fund				
		$ 50	1%	$ 95
Housing				
First Mortgage	$1,132			$1,132
Second Mortgage				
Real Estate Taxes				
Homeowners Insurance	$ 60			$ 60
Home Repairs				
Replace Furniture				
Other				
		$1,192	22%	$1,192
Utilities				
Electricity	$ 70			$ 70
Water	$ 35			$ 35

Category	Budgeted	Subtotal	% Take-Home	Amount Spent
Utilities (*cont.*)				
Gas	$ 60			$ 60
Phone	$ 80			$ 80
Trash				
Cable				
Computer On-line				
		$ 245	5%	245
Food				
Grocery	$ 500			$ 600
Restaurants	$ 50			$ 100
		$ 550	13%	$ 700
Transportation				
Car Payment 1	$ 335			$ 335
Car Payment 2				
Gas and Oil	$ 90			$ 90
Repairs and Tires	$ 83			$ 33
Car Insurance	$ 100			$ 100
License and Taxes	$ 10			$ 10
Car Replacement				
		$ 618	12%	$ 568

Continued on next page

Category	Budgeted	Subtotal	% Take-Home	Amount Spent
Clothing				
Children	$ 75			$ 75
Adults	$ 150			$ 100
Cleaning/Laundry	$ 65			$ 65
		$ 290	5%	$ 240
Medical/Health				
Disability Insurance				
Health Insurance	$ 300			$ 300
Doctor Bills	$ 80			$ 80
Dentist	$ 45			
Optometrist				
Drugs	$ 10			$ 10
Other				
		$ 435	8%	$ 390
Personal				
Life Insurance	$ 70			$ 70
Child Care				
Baby-sitter	$ 40			$ 40
Toiletries	$ 50			$ 50
Cosmetics	$ 20			$ 20

Category	Budgeted	Subtotal	% Take-Home	Amount Spent
Personal (*cont.*)				
Hair Care	$ 50			$ 50
Education/Adult				
School Tuition				
School Supplies	$ 100			$ 100
Child Support				
Alimony				
Subscriptions				
Organization Dues	$ 25			$ 25
Gifts (Christmas)	$ 125			$ 125
Miscellaneous				
		$ 480	9%	$ 480
Blow $$				
		0	0%	0
Recreation				
Entertainment	$ 100			$ 50
Vacation				
		$ 100	1%	$ 50
Debts ($0, you hope)				
Visa 1	$ 200			200
Visa 2				

Continued on next page

Category	Budgeted	Subtotal	% Take-Home	Amount Spent
Debts (*cont.*)				
MasterCard 1	_____			_____
MasterCard 2	$148			$ 148
American Express	_____			_____
Discover Card	_____			_____
Gas Card 1	_____			_____
Gas Card 2	_____			_____
Dept. Store Card 1	_____			_____
Dept. Store Card 2	_____			_____
Finance Co. 1	_____			_____
Finance Co. 2	_____			_____
Credit Line	_____			_____
Student Loan 1	_____			_____
Student Loan 2	_____			_____
Other Bank Loan	$567			$ 567
Other _____	_____			_____
Other _____	_____			_____
		$ 915	_____	$ 915
GRAND TOTAL		$5,174		$5,350
−TOTAL INCOME		$5,350		$5,350
ZERO				

restaurant. We had no idea how high the prices were until we had been seated, and then we were too embarrassed to ask to leave."

"We tried to order conservatively," Emily said. "But when the bill arrived, the other couple said, 'Ah, let's just split it. It'll be easier than asking for separate checks.' What were we supposed to do?"

To make up for their overspending, the couple pulled $50 each from the car repairs and tires category, the adult clothing expenses, and the recreation category. Obviously, borrowing from one category to make up for spending in another isn't ideal. But you will make mistakes, which will call for midmonth adjustments. What's important is that, if you are married, you decide *with* your spouse what categories you will borrow from to pay for your mistake (no pulling from the clothing budget to make the car payment unless you have consulted your mate) *and* that your budget balance is zero at the end of the month. And remember, when you pull money out of one category to make up for over-spending in another, the money won't be there later. It's gone.

To their credit, Barry and Emily stuck to their budget in the other categories. They had planned well. They wouldn't need to revise their budget again until they paid off another debt or Barry found a higher-paying job.

During the next month, keep track of your spending in the form on pages 75–79. Fill in the "Budgeted" column. Then fill in what you spend as you go through the month.

Compare what you have spent with your original plan on page 48, and answer the following questions:

What did you adjust midmonth and by how much?

Item	Amount Over	Amount Under
_____	_____	_____
_____	_____	_____
_____	_____	_____
_____	_____	_____
_____	_____	_____
_____	_____	_____
_____	_____	_____

Was your overspending caused by lack of discipline or poor planning?

_____

_____

_____

What changes, if any, do you need to make to next month's budget? Take time now to revise your budget. You can use the additional budget form in the appendix, on page 260.

When common mistakes and seemingly unavoidable circumstances, like Barry and Emily's dining experience, trip you up and cause you to fall off your budget, it's easy to get discouraged. Don't let one lapse keep you from getting back on the budget, though. A journalist once asked Paul Harvey how he had become a success. His reply: "Every time I fall down, I get back up." Just because you make a mistake doesn't mean budgets don't work. It just means you are human. Sometimes you will blow it. The trick is to learn from your mistakes and find ways to keep from repeating them. Here are some prevalent budget traps to avoid.

"How Could I Say No?"

This was the trap Barry and Emily fell into when they went to dinner with their friends—not that they should have made a scene and walked out of the restaurant. Sometimes you just have to learn from your mistakes the hard way—stupid tax, I call it. What Barry and Emily learned was to call ahead, whenever possible, and find out whether they could afford the designated restaurant.

There's no point in budgeting if you don't plan to live by it. That means you have to plan ahead for special occasions. When friends invite you to go out, suggest places you know you can afford. If they insist on going somewhere out of your price range, you will have to humble yourself and tell them the truth—that you have chosen to live on a budget and what they want to do is beyond your means. Then, offer an alternative solution. For example, you may say, "We can't go with you there, but why don't you meet us at (you name it) for dessert later? Or come over for a cup of coffee after we've put the kids down for the night?"

Your Monthly Cash-Flow Plan

Category	Budgeted	Subtotal	% Take-Home	Amount Spent
Charitable Gifts	_____			_____
		_____	_____	_____
Savings				
Emergency Fund	_____			_____
Retirement Fund	_____			_____
College Fund	_____			_____
		_____	_____	_____
Housing				
First Mortgage	_____			_____
Second Mortgage	_____			_____
Real Estate Taxes	_____			_____
Homeowners Insurance	_____			_____
Home Repairs	_____			_____
Replace Furniture	_____			_____
Other _____	_____			_____
		_____	_____	_____
Utilities				
Electricity	_____			_____
Water	_____			_____

Category	Budgeted	Subtotal	% Take-Home	Amount Spent
Utilities (*cont.*)				
Gas	_____			_____
Phone	_____			_____
Trash	_____			_____
Cable	_____			_____
Computer On-line	_____			_____
		_____	_____	_____
Food				
Grocery	_____			_____
Restaurants	_____			_____
		_____	_____	_____
Transportation				
Car Payment 1	_____			_____
Car Payment 2	_____			_____
Gas and Oil	_____			_____
Repairs and Tires	_____			_____
Car Insurance	_____			_____
License and Taxes	_____			_____
Car Replacement	_____			_____
		_____	_____	_____

Category	Budgeted	Subtotal	% Take-Home	Amount Spent
Clothing				
Children	————			————
Adults	————			————
Cleaning/Laundry	————			————
		————	————	————
Medical/Health				
Disability Insurance	————			————
Health Insurance	————			————
Doctor Bills	————			————
Dentist	————			————
Optometrist	————			————
Drugs	————			————
Other ————————	————			————
		————	————	————
Personal				
Life Insurance	————			————
Child Care	————			————
Baby-sitter	————			————
Toiletries	————			————
Cosmetics	————			————

Category	Budgeted	Subtotal	% Take-Home	Amount Spent
Personal (*cont.*)				
Hair Care	_____			_____
Education/Adult	_____			_____
School Tuition	_____			_____
School Supplies	_____			_____
Child Support	_____			_____
Alimony	_____			_____
Subscriptions	_____			_____
Gifts (Christmas)	_____			_____
Miscellaneous	_____			_____
		_____	_____	_____
Blow $$	_____			_____
		_____	_____	_____
Recreation				
Entertainment	_____			_____
Vacation	_____			_____
		_____	_____	_____
Debts ($0, you hope)				
Visa 1	_____			_____
Visa 2	_____			_____

Category	Budgeted	Subtotal	% Take-Home	Amount Spent
Debts (*cont.*)				
MasterCard 1	_____			_____
MasterCard 2	_____			_____
American Express	_____			_____
Discover Card	_____			_____
Gas Card 1	_____			_____
Gas Card 2	_____			_____
Dept. Store Card 1	_____			_____
Dept. Store Card 2	_____			_____
Finance Co. 1	_____			_____
Finance Co. 2	_____			_____
Credit Line	_____			_____
Student Loan 1	_____			_____
Student Loan 2	_____			_____
Other _____	_____			_____
Other _____	_____			_____
Other _____	_____			_____
	_____	_____		_____
GRAND TOTAL	_____			_____
–TOTAL INCOME	_____			_____
ZERO	_____			_____

Remember, learning to say no to yourself is as important as learning to say no to others. There will be hundreds, even thousands, of opportunities for you to "make an exception" to your budget. "Just this time" is the best friend of "broke." Learn to say no.

"When Did I Spend That?"

When Kit made her first budget, she allowed only $300 a year for school supplies for the teenage daughter who was still in high school. (Her college-age daughter was able to buy her books and other supplies out of her father's monthly support check.) She thought that was more than enough to buy books at the beginning of the year and a few extra supplies in the middle of the year. What she didn't take into account was the cost of tickets to school football games and plays, class projects, and class parties. When she went back and added in these expenses, she determined school supplies cost from $500 to $600 a year, enough to blow a budget every month.

Unless you are temporarily cutting out spending on a few categories, as Barry and Emily did in their initial budget in chapter 3, you should try to budget an amount for every category. Remember, be real—no denial. It's one thing to try to trim your budget so you can get out of debt or save some extra money. It's another to be unrealistic about how much it takes to live. You will need clothes; you will want to have a little fun every now and then. So don't overlook those categories. Budget for them.

You Don't Do It Together

Only two months into their marriage, J. G. noticed that Jill had charged several hundred dollars on their credit cards, buying furniture and knickknacks for the house they were renting. He asked her to cut back on her spending, but the next month, there were even more charges—this time for clothes.

Having watched his own parents lose a business and declare bankruptcy, J. G. suddenly feared that Jill's spending would put them in a similar position. So he decided it was time to "take charge of matters." He created a budget and handed it to her. "This is it," he said. "This is what you have to spend on groceries and clothing."

"You're nuts," Jill declared. "You have no clue how much things cost. How can I live by some numbers you've just pulled out of the air? Besides, I work and contribute to the household income. I don't need you to dictate to me what I can spend."

"Just let me handle this area," J. G. said. "I'm a banker, for crying out loud. I think I know more about money than you."

This was a classic case of budget abuse. Afraid of Jill's shopping habits and unable to communicate his concerns, J. G. dictated the terms of the budget to Jill and expected her to fall in line. Like any healthy person, however, Jill rebelled and the budget crashed.

It takes the entire family to create a written cash-flow plan that works. Both spouses have to work together, *before the month begins*, agreeing on how much is realistic to spend on food, clothing, date nights. Even teenagers can participate by contributing their ideas of what they need for fun and for extracurricular activities.

How Are You Doing?

Perhaps you haven't been on your new budget long enough to fall off. If you *have* had trouble sticking to your budget in the past, however, then consider the statements below. Which, if any, describes you?

____ I can't say no—to myself or anyone else for that matter.
____ Necessary expenses usually crash my budget.
____ My husband/wife dictates the budget to me.

Committing to live by your budget, saying no to yourself, and becoming realistic about how much you need to live on are tasks you can typically perform on your own, or, if necessary, with a little help from a financial buddy. Getting on the same financial page with your spouse is another issue. If you just can't seem to communicate with your spouse about financial matters, that may signal bigger problems. Don't be afraid to call a pastor or counselor for outside help.

The Envelope System

One way to make sure you don't overspend is to get on the envelope system. Here's how it works: Let's say you budget $600 for groceries, eating out, and toiletries. If you are like most people, you write a check at the grocery store, use a credit card at the restaurant, and write another check at the drugstore. At the end of the month, you look back and realize you spent $700—$100 over budget. On the envelope system, however, you pay for certain items with cash instead of with checks or credit cards. So, using the example above, you would cash a check for $600 on payday, then put the money into three envelopes marked "Groceries," "Restaurants," and "Toiletries." Then, as you need to buy any of those items, you take the money from those envelopes.

In addition to helping you keep track of how much you are spending, the envelope system helps you control your spending. You will almost never spend more than your budget allows: If the money is there, you know you have it to spend. No more credit cards, frequent checks, and frequent ATM withdrawals. It hurts more to pay with cash than it does to sign a check or a credit card receipt, which will make you think twice about spending the money in the first place.

Expenses to pay for with the envelope system include:

Grocery	Toiletries
Restaurants	Baby-sitter
Gas and Oil	Cosmetics
Car Repairs and Tires	Hair Care
Clothing	Blow Money
Laundry/Cleaning	Entertainment

You can also use the envelope system to help manage your small savings. For example, if you set aside $83 a month for car repairs, maintenance, and tires, you can either deposit that into a savings account or keep the money in an envelope. Then the money is available when you need it. Keep in mind, you are not sticking to your budget if you are robbing one envelope to pay for an item from another category. Don't use your entertainment money to buy a gift, for example. You will regret it later and want to rob another envelope to pay for entertainment. The result will be a snowball of overspending. The one exception to this rule is if you are just starting the program and you have a major expense, such as your car breaking down. Use whatever money you have saved in your emergency fund to foot the bill first. Then, if you *have* to, you can borrow from one of the "fun" categories, such as entertainment or restaurants.

Take time now to label twelve envelopes with the categories listed above. You may want to create envelopes for other categories, such as gifts, also. Use your allocated spending plan on page 57 to help you determine how much cash to put in each envelope. Barry and Emily decided, for example, to cash a check for groceries twice a month, in accordance with the amounts they had budgeted for in their allocated spending plan. Each time, they put the $250 in the "Grocery" envelope and used it for the next two weeks.

When you evaluate your spending at the end of the month, take time to consider also how the envelope system worked for you. Did you make it through the month without borrowing money from one envelope to pay for another category? How can you stick to the system better next month?

Some people find that they need to add envelopes for other categories. One woman I taught liked to entertain friends, but she didn't create an "Entertainment" envelope the first month she went on the system, nor did she budget for "Entertainment." As a result, she wound up borrowing from the "Restaurant" and "Grocery" envelopes and going over budget. The next month, she added an "Entertainment" envelope and made sure she budgeted for that category. Now she has more fun and no guilt.

Proper Care, Feeding, and Maintenance of Your Budget

Like an automobile, your budget needs periodic checkups and maintenance to keep your finances performing well and your household running smoothly. Make it a practice to review your income sources and update your budget one or two nights before the beginning of each month. If you are married, make an appointment to do this with your spouse and write it on the calendar.

A good plan changes. Today you may have a car payment. Next month, you may not. Your goals also change from time to time. When your kids go to college, for example, you may decide to increase your vacation savings and save less for the furniture fund.

As part of your monthly budget ritual, take time to balance your checkbook. A critical part of keeping your finances in order and your budget working, this task isn't always as easy as it seems. The moment you give in to the impatient line behind you in the grocery store and put off recording your check, the trouble starts. By the time you get home, you have forgotten about it; the next day you record another check but forget to bring the balance forward. Suddenly, you are an overdraft waiting to happen.

If you have trouble recording your checks, try using duplicate checks. Most banks sell carbon checks so you automatically record your check as you write it. You still have to carry your balance forward and reconcile your statement, but it helps you recall the details of each check you write.

Maintaining your budget and keeping your checkbook balanced will help you as you begin taking the next step in regaining control of your finances: dumping debt.

The Peace Track

Baby Step Checkup

You are only two chapters away from taking the second baby step, but you won't be able to move forward if you haven't completed baby step 1. So take time now to set some savings goals so you can accumulate $1,000 in your emergency fund if you haven't already completed the step. Have you already looked for additional work? What about cutting back on your entertainment spending for a month or two? Pay only the minimum balances on all of your bills until you have saved $1,000.

Baby Step	Done	Action Needed to Complete	Date
1. Save $1,000 in an emergency fund.			

Norman Vincent Peale said, "Plan your work for today and every day; then work your plan." Part of your financial plan is the budget you have just created. Make one of your goals this week to plan how you will spend your time; then commit to follow through on those plans.

Weekly Goals

	Goal	Date
Spiritual		
Relational		
Physical		
Mental		

FIVE

What Kind of Debt
Have You Bought?

"BEING ON A BUDGET has been great for us," Emily told the FPU class. "We have been able to control our spending and even start saving for our emergency fund. But we've also realized we're going to have to get out of debt if we ever plan to get ahead."

"It doesn't sound like getting out of debt is the key to getting ahead for you and Barry," Dennis spoke up. "Debt is supposed to be a sound way to establish credit. The only way you two will get ahead is by making more money."

Like many Americans, Dennis bought into the prevailing American philosophy that debt is good—it's the American way. Sure, he wanted to pay off his credit cards so the collectors would quit calling, but he saw debt as an asset. That's because borrowing money enabled him to invest in everything from a house to a once-in-a-lifetime business partnership. Dennis believed Visa U.S.A. chief economist Dr. Thomas A. Layman when he was quoted in the February 27, 1997, issue of *CardTrak*, a consumer newsletter about credit cards: "The wide availability of personal consumer credit is vital to the U.S. economy. Consumer spending accounts for roughly two-thirds of the nation's gross domestic product. Output and employment would *suffer* if there were a diminution in the wide availability of consumer credit." What else would you expect a Visa economist to say?

Dr. Layman had it wrong. Dennis had it wrong. Barry and Emily were *right*. You can develop a cash-flow plan and even start saving in your emergency fund, which you began in chapter 2. But, contrary to popular belief, you won't get ahead as long as you stay in debt and continue borrowing money.

Take some time now to think about what it would be like if you had no debt. Look at your monthly cash-flow plan on page 74. What percentage of your income goes toward paying creditors each month?_____
If you didn't have that debt, how much could you save every month?_____
How much could you give away?_____
How much would you have to earn if you had no payments? To calculate the figure, subtract the total of your debts, page 78, from the grand total. _____

Plastic Peril

Despite what Visa U.S.A.'s Dr. Layman says, personal credit is one of the most insidious products sold in America today. While banks and other financial institutions pump millions of dollars into marketing credit cards, consumers snatch them up to the tune of more than 43 million Discover cards, 33 million Citicorp cards, 23 million AT&T Visa cards, 25 million American *Excess* cards, and 26 million Sears cards. And the numbers continue to soar as companies successfully target new markets, such as small businesses and college and high school students. (Remember that college is when Dennis got into trouble with credit cards.) That may be good news for the credit card companies, but it is the beginning of the end for many consumers.

At the rate of seven cards each, the average consumer has not bought "more power," as one credit card advertisement suggests, but *perceived* plastic prosperity. You may appear prosperous, but, in fact, you are digging your own debt grave. In 1996, the American Bankers Association reported that 3.6 percent of accounts were delinquent—that's a record-setting 10.9 million accounts. And personal bankruptcies skyrocketed to a ten-year high of 1.1 million, with credit card debt being cited as one of the primary reasons for the bankruptcies.

It's easy to lose control of your spending when you use credit cards because you see no cash pass from your hand, so you don't feel the pain of spending. Instead, you feel glamorous and fun, and you wind up buying "stuff" you would never buy if you were paying cash. Studies show, for example, that you spend almost double on groceries when you charge them.

What's worse, when you finally get the bill, there are whopping double-digit interest rates levied against your purchases. The annual interest rates on credit cards hovered around 18 percent in 1995. That year, Americans charged almost $10 million on groceries alone. Assuming that none of the cards were paid up, consumers spent $1.8 million in interest for food. According to the January 1996 issue of *Consumer Reports* magazine, the average $1,828 credit card balance earned the issuers $329 a year in interest. For Citibank, interest charges added up to a hefty $4.5 million.

You can overcome the peril of plastic in one easy snip. That's right: Cut them up. In chapter 6, you will perform plastic surgery.

Wake-up Call!

Seventy-two percent of credit cards have variable rates, which means your debts will go up if the rates do. And the new interest rates are exacted against the entire balance, not just the new purchases. Only 17 percent of cardholders realize their rates are variable, however.

The Credit Card Test

Note: If you do not own a credit card, you do not need to take this test. (Do not get a credit card to take the test.)

If you own a credit card, look at last month's bill and determine which budget categories you used it for. Groceries? Clothing? Now, take the average amount you spent on one category and write that figure below.

For the next month, use the envelope system for that category. Put the amount of money you have budgeted for that category in an envelope and only buy that category with the cash in the envelope. At the end of the month, record below how much you spent.

How do the two compare?

Look at your credit card purchases for the past year. How much did you pay in interest for the year?

On a separate sheet of paper or with a calculator, determine how much you would have paid if you had bought the items with cash. Write the amount in the space below.

Most people spend less when paying with cash than when paying with a credit card or writing a check. If you haven't started using the envelope system, resolve to get on it this month. It really isn't worth the extra money you pay in interest to continue using your credit cards.

The Loan from HEL

Home equity loans increased 140 percent from 1987 to 1995. In 1995, more than $335 billion was loaned via home equity loans. Bankers call them HELs, but I think they just left off the other L.

Home equity loans are deceptively attractive. You think you are getting a good deal because current tax laws allow you to write off the interest on the loan. For example, if you are in the 30 percent tax bracket, you would owe $3,000 on $10,000 of income. But if you have $10,000 worth of interest on a loan, you can avoid paying the tax. The problem: You still owe the bank $7,000 in interest, not to mention the fact that you still have to pay back the principal.

Congratulations! You just went into debt because it was a "good deal." Amazing what a tax-law change followed by a little marketing will do to our sensibilities.

In addition to being a bad deal, home equity loans are risky. When you take out your loan, you offer your home as collateral. That means if you can't pay the loan, the bank can force you to sell your home to raise the cash or the bank can simply take your home from you in a foreclosure. Knowing you could lose your home probably makes that new furniture or exotic cruise a lot less appealing, right?

Have you taken out a home equity loan? What prompted you to do so?

_____

_____

How much are you paying in interest by taking out a HEL? How much less would you have paid for the same item if you had bought it with cash? List the amounts below:

Item	Amount	Interest
Cash Purchase	_____	0
Loan	_____	_____

How long would you have had to save to pay for your purchase in cash?

_____

Car Loans

Financial management rule number one: Never borrow on a depreciating asset. Unless you have short terms—three years or less—on a car, its value typically drops faster than the loan balance, which puts you in a precarious position. What will happen, for example, if you are laid off a year after financing an $18,000 car for six years at 13 percent? The car is only worth $13,000 now, but you still owe $16,800. When you owe more than an item's value, you are "upside down" in the loan. You can't make your $327 monthly payments and you can't sell the car for what you owe. So the finance company repossesses it and sells it for $9,000. (Repossession companies always sell cars below wholesale.) That means you still owe $7,800 on the car. If you are lucky, you can settle this debt with the finance company by making payments. But do you really want to pay for a car you no longer own?

One of the fastest ways to get into debt is buying a new car. One of the fastest ways to get out of debt is selling that new car. That's what Barry and Emily found out when they sold Barry's car and bought a $2,500 clunker instead. Their only mistake was not selling Emily's car too.

Take time now to consider whether you need to get out of your car loan. First, determine how much the car is worth now as well as what you owe on it. (You can call the bank to help you find these numbers, buy a National Automobile Dealers Association (NADA) book from your local bookstore, or find an NADA book at the local library.) Record the amounts in the space provided. There are spaces for two cars.

Model	Value	Debt

If you find you are upside down in the loan, plan to sell the car today and buy a used car for a lesser amount—say, $2,000. At the worst, you can sell the car for its value. What you still owe on the new car after selling it plus what you spend on a used car will likely be much less than your current car debt. You may lose a new car, but you'll gain a much more manageable debt.

The Lease

According to *Consumer Reports* magazine, the most expensive way to purchase an auto is to lease it. Why do dealers push leases and financing? The typical new car sale only nets the dealer $82, but if you lease it, the dealer's profit is between $1,000 and $1,300. Some of the big car companies are responding to consumer pressure and lowering the rates of their monthly leases. But still, you are paying a lot of money every month to not own anything at the end of your term.

Possibly the worst feature of most leases is that you are trapped for the term of the lease. Since most leases run five to seven years and most families trade cars more often than that, you are stuck with owning a car you don't want or having to find a way to get out of your lease. Often, you can trade cars at the dealership and get out of the lease for a penalty. But you pay the premium.

If you are currently leasing a car, read your contract and see what provisions are there for getting out of the lease. Ask the financing company what the "buyout" on the lease is—that is, how much it would cost to buy the car now, before the term of the lease is up. Similar to a loan payoff, the buyout may be more than the car is worth. For example, you may be able to buy out a lease for $17,000, but the car's value may only be $15,000. Even so, you are only $2,000 upside down in the loan, whereas you may lose more if you continue to make the lease payments and wind up at the end of the five- to seven-year term with no car at all. Buyer beware: The dealership may try to scare you by telling you you can't get out of your lease, but most leases include an out.

Debt Consolidation Loans

The first three letters of the word *consolidation* say it all: It's a *con*. The pitch from the finance and thrift companies is this: Let us loan you the money so you can pay off all your loans; then, you'll have just one bill—with a lower payment—to pay. Sounds great, right? When Kit started noticing her bills adding up, she explored the possibility of taking out a consolidation loan. First, she recorded her debts (see top of page 93).

The finance company offered to reduce Kit's monthly payments to $550 for thirty-six months. But her cost plus interest would have been $19,800. The

Debt	Balance	Monthly Minimum Payment	Interest Rate
Visa	$1,200	$ 25	18%
MasterCard	$1,700	$ 45	18%
Gas Card	$ 600	$ 80	18%
Car	$6,500	$270	12%
Doctor	$ 400	$100	18%
Furniture	$3,500	$175	15%
TOTAL	$13,900	$695	

result: Not only would she have ended up paying more than she owed to begin with, she would also have paid over a longer period of time.

The bigger problem with the consolidation loan is that it treats the symptoms instead of the problem. Getting a loan to get out of debt may help you keep a few lenders at bay, but it also keeps you addicted to spending and borrowing. To get out of debt, you need a plan, a method of repayment that will help you gain the discipline not to get into debt again. The debt snowball, which we talk about in chapter 6, provides such a plan.

Before you get a consolidation loan, figure out how much it will cost you. Use the chart below to record and total your debts and monthly minimums. Compare that with what you will pay over the life of the loan you are about to get.

Debt	Balance	Monthly Minimum Payment	Interest Rate
_____	_____	_____	_____
_____	_____	_____	_____
_____	_____	_____	_____
_____	_____	_____	_____
_____	_____	_____	_____
_____	_____	_____	_____
TOTAL			

Don't wind up paying more than you owe. In the next chapter, we will talk about how to use the debt snowball to repay your debts. If you already have a debt consolidation loan, you can pay extra on the loan every month or pay one additional payment a year. The extra money will go directly to paying off the principal, which will help pay off the loan faster.

The Friendly Loan

It's not marketed to you by retailers or financial institutions, but the friendly loan causes so many problems it's worth mentioning here. The best way to strain a relationship is to borrow money from a friend or relative. A biblical principle first described in the Old Testament explains why: The borrower is the servant to the lender (Proverbs 22:7). You become obligated to your lenders; and if you can't repay them, your friendship will likely be destroyed.

Co-signing a loan for a friend is as bad as handing him the money. Think of what you are doing: The trained, professional moneylender has decided your friend should not borrow, but you, in your infinite wisdom, know better. So you sign for him. When the loan goes bad, who will the bank look for? You. The bank knows your friend (or child or sibling) doesn't have the money.

Have you ever borrowed from or loaned money to a friend or relative? What was the purpose of the loan?

_____

_____

Have you ever co-signed a loan? What was the loan for?

_____

_____

How did your relationship change with your lender or borrower after that, if at all?

_____

_____

_____

_____

If You *Have* to Go into Debt . . .

The one kind of debt that may be worthwhile is a regular home loan, better known as a mortgage. The interest rates and terms are about the best loan rates available to the consumer. Just make sure you borrow on short terms—fifteen years or less—and at low rates. We will look at how much you can save by buying a less expensive home over a shorter term in chapter 12. But before getting a mortgage, let me alert you to two real estate caveats:

1. *Beware the well-meaning, well-trained realtors who will sell you all you can afford on a thirty-year mortgage.* They get paid on a percentage of the sales price, not on how much you save. Your loan officer may well tell you that you qualify for more than you *want* to spend, but just because you qualify doesn't mean you should take the bank's money. Buy less house over a shorter term so you have less debt to carry.
2. *Beware the adjustable rate mortgages, or ARMs.* These mortgages normally adjust annually based on indices, such as the one-year Treasury bills (T-bills) or on the eleventh district cost of funds index for the Federal Home Loan Bank Board. The T-bill is the more volatile of the two, but neither is acceptable in terms of risk. Worse, according to the *Wall Street Journal*, many financial institutions "forget" to lower the rate (strange how they never "forget" to raise it).

Wake-up Call!

If you have too many open credit card accounts, even with zero balances, the mortgage company will count it against you when qualifying you for a mortgage.

We will talk about how much house you can afford and how to pay off your home early in chapters 6 and 12. For now, take time to review your borrowing habits.

List the types of loans you currently have: credit cards, a HEL, a consolidation loan.

1. _____
2. _____
3. _____
4. _____
5. _____

What sold you on these various loans? Describe in the space below how you found out about these kinds of loans and how you decided to borrow.

_____
_____
_____
_____

What sold you on the last credit card you signed up for? How did you find out about the card? What "benefits" did the card or company offer that appealed to you?

_____
_____
_____

Credit card offers come in the mail almost every day. Study the next offer you receive, noticing how the company sells their product. In the space below, list the catchphrases the company uses to market the card.

1. _____
2. _____
3. _____
4. _____

Look over the answers to these questions. If you had to do it again, what would you change?

_____

_____

If someone were to offer you a credit card, a HEL, a lease, or a consolidation loan today, how would you respond?

_____

_____

You may remember the story in *Financial Peace* about the Missouri woman named Linda Welch, who thought she had cancer. Having watched her mother die of the same agonizing disease, she couldn't bear to endure it herself or leave her children alone in the world. So she decided to kill herself and her children. The sad irony was that she didn't have cancer. Instead, the autopsy revealed she had the flu and strep throat.

No matter how passionately you believe it to be true, acting on incorrect information can be catastrophic at worst and painful at best. As long as you keep borrowing money and living with debt, you are committing financial suicide. At the worst, you could wind up losing your family and everything you own. At the least, it will take you several months to dig your way out of trouble.

Before you proceed to chapter 6 and start getting out of debt, take time to "pump yourself up," as *Saturday Night Live* actor Dana Carvey would say. One key to your success in dumping debt is to *get mad!* (Let me hear you growl.) A good dose of healthy anger—emotion, not logic—will give you the necessary energy to keep going. Reread the debt marketing tactics you listed on page 96. Don't they make you mad? Now think about the pain people endure because of debt—the lost homes and broken families. What about your own situation?

When was the last time you were stressed out because of debt?

_____

_____

_____

_____

Describe the last time you felt angry at debt. When was it? Why were you angry?

_____

_____

_____

_____

What will it take to make you mad enough never to borrow money again?

_____

_____

_____

_____

When you feel fired up, you are ready to move on to chapter 6 and to start digging your way out of debt.

The Peace Track

Baby Step Checkup

By now, you are five weeks into the Financial Peace program. Some folks have saved $1,000 in their emergency fund. Others need more time. That's okay. Take time to review your savings strategies. Are you consistently putting something away in a bank savings or money market account each week? Even $5 a week will help. You may have to cut out blow money, recreational spending, even saving for a vacation for a month or two until you can build up your emergency fund.

What about the budget? Are you spending only what you have allotted for each category? Are you using the envelope system?

Sticking to your budget and paying cash for everything will help you gain the discipline necessary to save for emergencies.

Record your progress in the following chart.

Baby Step	Done	Action Needed to Complete	Date
1. Save $1,000 in an emergency fund.			

Make one of your goals for next week to review all of your loans. What can you do to speed up the payments on your debts? Are there any debts you can afford to pay off?

Weekly Goals

	Goal	Date
Spiritual		
Relational		
Physical		
Mental		

· SIX ·

Reversal of Fortune: Dump Debt

"DENNIS, IF YOU REALLY WANT to keep from getting into trouble again, you're going to have to cut up your credit cards," I told him after FPU one evening. Barry, Emily, J. G., Jill, and Kit were standing nearby listening.

"All of them?" His voice cracked.

"All of them."

"B-B-But Dave," he protested. "I've got to have *one* credit card, just for making hotel and airline reservations when I travel."

"No you don't." The others shifted uncomfortably as Dennis looked increasingly flustered.

"But I've learned my lesson. I'll only use them for travel and cashing checks."

Like Dennis, most people come slightly unglued when I challenge them to cut up their credit cards. They tell me they *need* the cards, they have learned their lesson, and they will pay off their balances every month from now on. Don't kid yourself. I have seen too much pain that proves otherwise.

It all starts innocently enough. You get your first credit card as a rite of passage into adulthood. Then, suddenly, like many of the people who walk into my office for counsel, you owe $23,000, $44,000, $63,000, $123,000 on your cards.

One couple I counseled divorced after fifteen years of marriage because of credit card debt. They had never been a day late on their payments until a few months before they came to see me. Then the husband was laid off. Instead of cutting back on their spending, the couple maintained their two-income lifestyle, accumulating $50,000 in credit card debt. They ended up losing everything they owned; and though they tried to start over, the financial stress and the resulting breakdown of trust between them destroyed their marriage.

Please don't tell me you can control your plastic. Most of us can't. The only way to avoid financial trouble—large or small—is to cut up the credit cards and avoid debt altogether. In this chapter, you will learn how to get out and stay out of debt. These exercises may be some of the toughest you complete in the entire workbook. It won't be easy to give up the credit card and debt habit, especially if that is how you are used to making ends meet. If you need help completing any of the exercises—or if you need to be held accountable to complete them—call your financial buddy.

Plastic Surgery

Get ready to perform plastic surgery on your cards. That's right, you are going to take out your cards and a pair of scissors, and cut up those cards. There are at least three good reasons everyone needs this operation:

1. Seventy-eight percent of people don't pay off their credit card each month, even though they swear they will.
2. Consumers spend 12 percent more on general purchases than they would if they used cash for the same purchases.
3. Consumers spend 54 percent more on food (eating out and groceries) than they would if they used cash.

Dennis thought he had learned his lesson and could handle the credit cards. When I confronted Barry about his cards, he told me he needed them because he had depended on them each time he had been laid off. He didn't want to use them, but he was afraid to get rid of them. Jill wanted to keep her cards so she could order catalog items by phone. And Kit thought she needed a credit card to cash checks and charge her business expenses. All of them had overlooked an alternative: Use a debit card.

Most merchants who accept Visa and MasterCard credit cards also accept their debit card counterparts. In fact, you don't even have to specify whether you are giving a debit or a credit card number. The merchant treats them the same; the difference is that the payments come out of your checking account the same night, as if you were using an ATM card. I have a personal and business debit card for convenience (there, you can still enjoy the convenience of plastic). However, I only use them for travel because you spend less when you use cash.

What do you purchase now that you can't purchase with a debit card or cash?

_____

_____

Remember the results of your credit card test from chapter 5? If not, go back and look at page 89. When did you spend more: using cash or credit cards?

_____

_____

What's holding you back from cutting up your credit cards? List three good reasons you can't let go.

1. _____
2. _____
3. _____

See, you can't come up with really good reasons not to get rid of your credit cards. So now is the time: Take out your credit cards—including the gas cards, the department store cards, the Visa and Discover cards, and all the cards hidden in your drawers, closets, and kitchen cupboard—and a pair of scissors. Deliberately cut each card in half or in quarters. (You may have to call your financial buddy to help you walk through this process.) Then throw them away; or, better, put them in a jar to remind you never to borrow again. You can also mail the cut-up cards to me if you don't want them: Dave Ramsey, The Lampo Group, Suite 257W, Brentwood, Tennessee 37027. And whatever you do, don't open another charge account *ever* again.

Wake-up Call!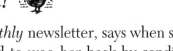

Mary Hunt, author of the *Cheapskate Monthly* newsletter, says when she first canceled her credit cards, the issuers tried to woo her back by sending her cards, flowers, and chocolates. Watch what happens after you perform plastic surgery.

Baby Step 2: The Debt Snowball

"I already feel more in control of my money now that I've cut up my credit cards," Kit said. "But plastic surgery alone won't get me out of debt. Sometimes I get so overwhelmed just looking at the piles of bills. How am I ever going to pay it all?"

There is an extremely useful tool you can use to help you figure out how to tackle a big pile of bills, and it's baby step 2:

Pay off all debt but the mortgage using the "debt snowball."

First, I asked Kit to write down all her debts (see top of page 104). Note that the list includes the interest rate on each outstanding bill.

Logic would suggest that Kit attack the largest bill or the one with the highest rate of interest first. But then, if we were using logic, we wouldn't be in debt right now. Paying off the largest debts or the ones with the highest interest rates first is a long, grueling process. A more rewarding way to repay debt is to start with the smallest bills first, regardless of the interest rate, and work up to paying off the largest bills. That way, you can see some of your debt disappear quickly, which gives you a feeling of success—like losing five

Item	Balance	Payment	Interest Rate
MasterCard	$ 1,700	$ 45	15%
Gas Card	$ 600	$ 80	12%
Furniture	$ 3,500	$175	15%
Doctor	$ 400	$100	7%
Car	$ 6,500	$270	10%
Visa	$ 1,200	$ 25	18%
House Payment	$80,000	$640	8%

pounds the first week of a diet. A series of successes will motivate you to keep going until you are completely debt-free.

The plan of attack, then, is to list your debts on a sheet of paper in order from smallest to largest. Using this strategy, Kit's list of bills looked like this:

Kit's Debt Snowball

Item	Balance	Payment
Doctor	$ 400	$100
Gas Card	$ 600	$ 80
Visa	$ 1,200	$ 25
MasterCard	$ 1,700	$ 45
Furniture	$ 3,500	$175
Car	$ 6,500	$270
House Payment	$80,000	$640

Pay the monthly minimums on every bill except the smallest. (If you can't afford to pay the monthly minimums, skip to the pro rata plan, on page 106.) If you have extra money, apply it to the smallest bill. Kit applied part of her quarterly bonus to the doctor's bill and paid it off the first month. You may be able to earn extra money by selling something or having a garage sale or working overtime. After paying off your smallest bill, apply its minimum monthly payment to the next largest bill on your list. *Do not* use the freed-up payment to buy a new dress or treat yourself to dinner out.

Kit applied the $100 doctor payment to her monthly gas card payment so she was paying $180 a month on the gas card. She paid the gas card off in month four. In month five, she added the $180 to the $25 minimum Visa payment and paid $205 on that bill. Continuing the process, Kit would be able to pay all of her bills except the mortgage by month twenty-four. Then she would have $1,335 to put toward house payments; or she could pay $1,000 a month on the house and start saving $335 a month toward a new car.

There are two requirements for the debt snowball to work: You have to keep up with your monthly payments, and you can't create any new debt. This means no overspending or borrowing money. If you stick to the program, you will soon be out of debt and ready to save to meet long-term goals.

Take time to organize your debts so you can use the debt snowball. In the space provided below, list your debts from smallest to largest, along with the monthly minimum payments.

Your Debt Snowball

Item	Balance	Payment

What can you do to pay off the smallest debt in the first or second month? Refer to your equity sheet on page 35 to see if there is something you can sell. In the space that follows, list your ideas and the amount of money you could make for each.

Item/Job	Amount
_____	_____
_____	_____
_____	_____
_____	_____

If you are unable to pay your creditors the minimum due each month, then you should use the pro rata plan. *Pro rata* means proportionately according to someone's fair share. The plan, then, organizes your payments so you are giving each creditor his or her share of your total debt. Here's how it works: Divide each individual debt by the total amount of debt. That gives you each debt's percentage of the total. Then, multiply the percentage by your disposable income, which is how much you have left after you pay for necessities (food, clothing, shelter, gasoline, utilities, insurance, school supplies). Let's use Kit's debts as an example. Her total debt, not including the house, is $13,900. The doctor's bill is 2.8 percent of that. Say, after paying for her necessities, she has about $800. She would then multiply .028 times $800 for a total of $22.40, which she would send to the doctor every month until she had paid the bill or she could afford to start paying monthly minimums. In order to figure out her pro rata payments, Kit would complete a chart that looks like the following:

Item	Total Payoff	÷	Total Debt	=	Percent	×	Disposable Income	=	New Payment
Doctor	$ 400	÷	$13,900	=	2.8%	×	$800	=	$ 22.40
Gas	$ 600	÷	$13,900	=	4.3%	×	$800	=	$ 34.40
Visa	$1,200	÷	$13,900	=	8.6%	×	$800	=	$ 68.80
MasterCard	$1,700	÷	$13,900	=	12.2%	×	$800	=	$ 97.60
Furniture	$3,500	÷	$13,900	=	25.2%	×	$800	=	$201.60
Car	$6,500	÷	$13,900	=	46.8%	×	$800	=	$374.40

Before you implement this plan, be sure you write each creditor and explain to them what you are about to do. Then send them a check attached to a copy of your budget and your pro rata sheet. The creditor may say he won't accept your payment, but do it anyway. When they see that you are consistently communicating and sending them something, most will leave you alone. I have had clients send as little as two dollars to each creditor and survive for years on this program.

Fill out the following pro rata plan if you are unable to make your monthly minimum payments.

Item	Total Payoff	÷	Total Debt	=	Percent	×	Disposable Income	=	New Payment
_____	_____	÷	_____	=	_____	×	_____	=	_____
_____	_____	÷	_____	=	_____	×	_____	=	_____
_____	_____	÷	_____	=	_____	×	_____	=	_____
_____	_____	÷	_____	=	_____	×	_____	=	_____
_____	_____	÷	_____	=	_____	×	_____	=	_____
_____	_____	÷	_____	=	_____	×	_____	=	_____
_____	_____	÷	_____	=	_____	×	_____	=	_____
_____	_____	÷	_____	=	_____	×	_____	=	_____

Steps to Jump-start Debt Repayment

Sometimes you have to generate extra income to repay your debt. Emily and Barry sold an antique; Kit used part of her bonus to pay off debt and get the snowball rolling. If your annual household income is less than $20,000, it's likely your paycheck barely covers your basic needs, much less the minimum payments on your bills. Here are some other steps you can take to increase your income.

   1. *Work overtime or take on a part-time job.* You may remember Barry took a job delivering newspapers at four o'clock in the morning. He worked

---

Wake-up Call!

Forty percent of Americans have not read a nonfiction book since their last day of formal education. It's time to turn off the television and put down the romance novels and improve your intellect so you can increase your earning power.

---

at that job for eight months, until he was able to get a higher-paying job. "He pretty much came in and went to bed, got up and went to work," Emily said.

There are plenty of opportunities for part-time jobs today, even if you have to work from home. You can take advantage of the home-based business boom. For example, find a company who will furnish you with a computer, and do database entry for them at night. Or offer your services as a baby-sitter, house cleaner, or lawn mower. You may also want to read some of the dozens of books that can give you ideas about the right home business for you or ways to earn a second income.

2. *Pray.* No kidding, it works!

3. *Improve your skills.* It will help qualify you for a higher-paying position. You can start by reading books and taking classes.

All you need is the will and the hope that you can do what's necessary to pull yourself out of the financial rut.

Take time now to brainstorm about what part-time jobs could help you to immediately increase your income. (Example: *Deliver pizza; data processing.*)

1. _____
2. _____
3. _____
4. _____
5. _____

Now, dream a little. Go to the library and research other jobs that sound interesting to you, or ask your personnel director what the salary range is for the level above yours. Let her know you are trying to improve yourself so you can qualify for a pay increase. Then, create an action plan. Decide what you need to do to pursue the job you want, and write the steps under the "Action" column. Set dates by which you will take those steps. (Example: *1. Find out who offers accounting courses and what they cost. 2. Talk to personnel director to see whether company will pay for continuing education. 3. Sign up for course. . . .*)

	Action	Date
1.	_____	_____
2.	_____	_____
3.	_____	_____
4.	_____	_____
5.	_____	_____

Plan to Resist

The debt snowball and the pro rata plan provide two workable solutions to debt. They make it possible for you to regain control of your finances while still paying for your basic needs. That is the only way you will keep from going bankrupt and get on the road to financial recovery. By getting angry at debt and taking the necessary steps, you will soon be ready to save and grow wealth for the future.

The Peace Track

Baby Step Checkup

If have completed baby step 1, you are ready to start working on the debt snowball. It will help you stay motivated if you have something to look forward to—a date you expect to pay off your first and second debts, for example. You can ask your banker for help figuring out how long it will take to pay them. Or you can use this simple method: For a one-year loan, divide the payoff, or what you still owe, by the current monthly payment and add one month (that accounts for interest). For a two- to three-year loan, divide the payoff by the monthly payment and add two months. That gives you an approximate idea of how many months you have until you have paid off the debt entirely.

Mark on your calendar the days you will pay those debts so you can celebrate. Keep your celebrations low-cost, of course. Have a picnic or create a special dinner at home.

Baby Step	Done	Action Needed to Complete	Date
1. Save $1,000 in an emergency fund.			
2. Pay off all debt but the mortgage with the "debt snowball."			

Dale Carnegie said, "You never achieve real success unless you like what you are doing." Some days you just have to tough out your job—hang in there and suffer through it—because you need the money to pay the bills and support the family. On the other hand, if you are never happy at work, maybe it's time to start asking yourself why. Include career research as one of your goals for the week. Plan to meet with a career counselor if you have no idea what you would like to do or with the director of personnel about what you can do to improve your salary.

Weekly Goals

	Goal	Date
Spiritual		
Relational		
Physical		
Mental		

SEVEN

Credit Cleanup

SOME PEOPLE KNOW what it's like to cringe with dread every time the phone rings because it might be a collector or creditor. Others have never had to endure that stress—and if that's you, you're lucky. Even if you are one of the lucky ones, don't skip this chapter. Making sure your credit is good is essential to your financial health and well-being. Potential employers often use credit reports as a character reference. And a credit report is required to get a mortgage.

The problem is that more than 50 percent of credit reports have errors. Someone else whose name or Social Security number is similar to yours may have bad credit that is inadvertently recorded on your file. If you don't know how to check your credit report and correct mistakes, you will never know there is a problem until it's too late. If you know you have bad credit, then you need a plan, a way to manage the one-eyed collection monsters who threaten to strike at your emotional nerves and suck you dry of hope and peace.

Manage the Monsters

It may sound harsh to call collection agents monsters, but they utilize some monstrous practices that can gnaw at your peace and eventually destroy your hope. One client told me that a collector called while she was in the shower and talked to her nine-year-old daughter. The agent told the child that if her mommy didn't pay the bills, then the sheriff was going to take the little girl's toys away.

The best way for you to pay your debts and manage the monsters is by creating a plan. As representatives of your creditors, the collection agents' job is to get you to pay them first. So they search for techniques that will move you to action. They try to evoke strong emotion in you so you forget you have other bills to pay, such as food, clothing, shelter, and transportation. They will push your anger, fear, shame, or guilt buttons. They will even try to befriend you, offering to "help" you get out of debt. As unlikely as it sounds, when the agents find a tactic that works, they record it on their computers so they can remember to use it again the next time they call.

Your job is to build four protective walls around you and your family by paying your necessities first—food, clothing, shelter, transportation. Let nothing interfere with those priorities. Then, *you* set the order of payment to your creditors. Don't allow creditors or collectors to reprioritize your life around themselves. Learn what tactics they use on you that work. Then harden yourself to their tricks. It's the only way you will win at their game.

In the space below, describe your experiences with creditors or collection agents. How have they tried to convince you to pay them?

_____

_____

_____

_____

Think about the times you have given in to their demands and sent them money. What tactics moved you to pay them? When they made you mad? When they befriended you or acted like they were helping you?

_____

_____

_____

_____

You are morally and legally responsible to pay your debts, but you are not obligated to pay them at the expense of your health or well-being. If you haven't completed chapter 6, go back and fill in the pro rata form on page 107. That is the best plan to use when collectors are hounding you and you can't make your monthly minimum payments. After you complete the form, write a letter to each creditor, explaining what you are doing. Attach your payment, a copy of the form (to show that he is getting his fair percentage of debt), and a copy of your budget to each letter.

You will always stay ahead of your creditors by calling them more than they call you and by sending them more paper than they send you. When they see you are consistent and that you pay when you say you will, most collectors will back off.

Know Your Legal Rights

Another way to manage the collection monsters is to know your legal rights. In 1977, Congress passed a law called the Federal Fair Debt Collection Practices Act to help protect you from unfair collectors. The act makes the following stipulations:

1. *Collectors can call only between the hours of 8:00 A.M and 9:00 P.M., unless you have given them permission to do otherwise.*
2. *You can keep creditors from calling you at work.* You should request this in writing, using the letter on page 116 as a sample. Be sure to send the letter by certified mail, return receipt requested. That way you will know the next time you get a call whether the creditor has received your letter and whether they are breaking the law by calling you.
3. *You can demand that creditors stop all contact except to notify you of legal proceedings.* Again, do this in writing. A sample letter is provided on page 117, but only use this as a last resort in the most extreme cases. Writing a cease-and-desist letter is a great way to make a creditor mad—not a good move when you are trying to work with them to settle

your debts. The preferred way to get rid of an obnoxious collector who keeps calling: hang up. I don't know many people who keep talking when the phone is in the cradle.

4. *Collectors and creditors cannot confiscate a bank account or garnishee (attach) wages without suing you and winning the case.* Threats to garnishee your wages are bluffs, so don't respond. Just reassure the creditor they will get their money when you have it.

Barry and Emily received so many collection calls before they came to a Financial Peace seminar that they finally stopped answering the phone. After they learned what their rights were and gained a better understanding of the collection business, their attitude changed. "We got over them," Barry said. "When you realize that these folks sit in a room and call hundreds of people every day—they're telemarketers basically—you take it less personally. They're just doing their job. Our job is to protect ourselves and our family."

Wake-up Call!

The average turnover rate for collection agents is ninety days. They don't love what they do either; they are simply trained salespeople. So don't be threatened by them.

If you are working with a creditor who persists in harassing you or who will not work with you to establish a payment plan, then you can, as a last resort, use the cease-and-desist letter on page 117.

Be sure to send the letter via certified mail, return receipt requested. Collection agencies are notorious for moving slowly and for "losing" letters. Your receipt provides proof that they received your notification, particularly if you plan to sue.

Sample Letter to Creditor

[Date] _____

From

_____

_____

_____

[To]

_____

_____

_____

RE: _____

Dear _____ ,

I am writing to request formally that your firm (or any agency hired by your firm) no longer contact me at my place of employment:

_____ .

My employer requests calls such as yours must cease. Under the terms of the 1977 Federal Fair Debt Collection Practices Act, I formally demand all such calls to my place of employment cease. You will please take note that this letter was sent by certified mail so I have proof that you are in receipt of this letter should legal action against you become necessary on this matter.

I am willing to pay the debt I owe you, and I will be in touch soon to work out arrangements.

Feel free to contact me at my home between _____ A.M. and _____ P.M. at the following number _____ or by mail at my home address:

_____

_____

Please give this matter the attention it deserves.

Sincerely,

_____

Sample Cease-and-Desist Letter

[Date] _____

From

_____

_____

_____

VIA: Certified Mail, Return Receipt Requested

[To]

_____

_____

_____

RE: _____

Dear _____:

You are hereby notified under provisions of Public Law 95-109, Section 805-C, the Federal Fair Debt Collection Practices Act, to hereby CEASE AND DESIST in any and all attempts to collect the above debt. Your failure to do so WILL result in charges being filed against you with the state and federal regulatory agencies empowered with enforcement.

Please be further warned that if ANY derogatory information is placed on any credit reports after receipt of this notice, it, too, will result in action being taken against you.

PLEASE GIVE THIS MATTER THE ATTENTION IT DESERVES.

Yours truly,

_____

So What If They Sue?

If you fail to start repaying your debts or to communicate with your creditors, they will eventually sue you. The sheriff's department will serve notice of the court date, usually ten days from the date of service. Then, any case for less than $10,000 will be tried in a general sessions, or small claims, court. The proceeding is informal, but don't expect to win. The deck is stacked in favor of the collection agency. One man I know lost a case on a debt he didn't even owe.

You do have the option to try to settle with the creditor or the attorney in writing anytime during the lawsuit. If you can't reach an agreement, you can file a "slow pay motion," called a pauper's oath in some states, with the court. This will allow you to pay payments on the debt.

Whether you are settling a lawsuit or trying to reason with your creditor before being sued, the primary goal is to stay in control of your household. Fear, shame, and guilt keep you out of control and unproductive. Your financial problems will put stress on your marriage and may make you unable to perform on the job. That is a formula for failure. So do everything you can to make sure that you pay your debts on your terms—*after* you take care of your necessities.

Take time now to plan how you will deal with the collection agents and creditors who may be calling you. Whom have you avoided lately? What do you need to do to reassure that agency or company that they will receive payment?

_____

_____

_____

Clean Up Your Credit

Even if you are financially healthy, you need to check your credit report every one to two years for inaccuracies. The Federal Fair Credit Reporting Act, which was also passed in 1977 and which regulates how credit bureaus interact with consumers and creditors, allows you to have mistakes on your credit report corrected. All you have to do is get your report and notify the credit bureau in writing of the problems.

There are agencies that will offer to clean up your credit for you for a $300 or $400 fee, but why pay money for something you can do yourself? Besides, there is an abundance of credit cleanup scams that offer to clear your report even of accurate information. The 1977 act allows only inaccurate information to be removed. Anyone who offers to remove accurate information is offering to help you break the law. Here are the steps to cleaning up your credit report.

Step 1. *Get a copy of your report by calling one of the three national credit bureaus, TRW, TransUnion, and CBI Equifax, as well as your local credit bureau.* The numbers for the national bureaus are listed in the appendix, on page 255. You will likely get an automated message instructing you to mail a check, along with the information on the form below. You can use the form on page 120, or create your own.

Step 2. *Interpret the report.* Once you receive the report, carefully peruse it to see if there are any errors. The payment history on your file is supplied by creditors with whom you have had an account during the last seven years (five years in New York) and includes both open and closed accounts. Some accounts may appear twice on the report. That's because a creditor has issued both a revolving and an installment account or because you moved and the creditor transferred your account and issued you a new account number. A revolving account is paid off in full every month; an installment account can be paid in small monthly minimum amounts.

Keep in mind:

- *A divorce decree does not release you from legal responsibility on any account with your name on it.* You must contact each creditor individually and seek release of your obligation.
- *Just because you pay off a debt doesn't mean your payment history will be removed.* Any activity on an account or any judgment filed against you stays on your report for seven years (five in New York State), except for Chapter 7 bankruptcies, which stay on your report for ten years.

REQUEST FOR FILE DISCLOSURE

_____
(Credit Bureau Address)

Reason for File Disclosure Request _____

Referred by _____ Was credit refused? ☐ Yes ☐ No

I hereby request the Credit Bureau to disclose to me the contents of my credit record. I understand that if I have been rejected for credit within the past sixty (60) days as the result of credit information contained in my credit record, there will be NO CHARGE for this disclosure. Otherwise, there will be an _____(fill in amount)_____ charge for an individual disclosure and a ____(fill in amount)____ charge for both me and my spouse.

Name _____ Phone No. _____

Spouse's Name _____

Present Address _____

City _____ State _____ Zip Code _____

Former Address _____

City _____ State _____ Zip Code _____

Date of Birth _____ Social Security No. _____

Employer _____

How long with current employer? _____ Position _____

Former Employment _____

Spouse's Date of Birth _____ Social Security No. _____

Spouse's Employment _____

How long with current employer? _____ Position _____

I hereby authorize the Credit Bureau to review my credit record with me, to make any necessary investigation of my credit transactions and to furnish to its subscribers reports based thereon. In consideration of its undertaking to make such an investigation, I authorize any business or organization to give full information and records about me. I am the person named above and I understand that Federal Law provides that a person who obtains information from a consumer reporting agency under false pretenses shall be fined not more than $5,000 or imprisoned no more than one year or both.

Signed _____ Date _____

Phone number _____ Ext. _____ where I can be reached during normal working hours.

AUTHORIZATION FOR DISCLOSURE OF SPOUSE'S CREDIT RECORD

I, _____, certify that I am presently married to _____, and am acting in his/her behalf in reviewing the credit record information concerning him/her maintained by the Credit Bureau.

Signed _____ Date _____

• *The balance on the file is not necessarily current.* Check it to make sure it was correct as of the date reported. If so, then it's not necessary to investigate the balance on that account.

Study the sample credit report on page 122 to help you understand your own report. The major categories of information recorded are the

• credit history section: includes both open and closed accounts;
• collection agency accounts: any accounts your creditors turned over to the collection agency;
• courthouse records: public-record items obtained from local, state, and federal courthouses;
• former addresses and employers;
• inquiries: businesses that have received your credit report in the last twenty-four months.

If you have owned credit cards in the past (you've cut them up now, of course), the report will show when your last activity on the card was and the status, or whether you have paid the amount due. A key for the type of account and the timeliness of payment appears at the bottom of the report, as shown, to help you crack the codes.

For example, the status of John Doe's Chase credit card is R5, which means it is 120 days past due. This isn't the first time he has been late paying bills for that card, however. The "prior paying history" line shows that he has been thirty days late three times, sixty days late four times, and ninety days late one time in the past—30(03) 60(04) 90+(01). The same line includes the two most recent delinquencies, along with the most severe delinquency, March 1996, ninety days late.

Be sure that all of the account numbers match those on your cards. (Dig up your old bills to check the numbers since you have cut up the cards.) If John Doe did not own a Chase card, account number 54229778, as shown on the report, then he would need to take the next step.

How to Read Your Credit File

I.D. Section
Your name, current address and other identifying information reported by your creditors.

The Name and Address of the office you should contact if you have any questions or disagreement with your credit file

The Name and Address of the office you should contact if you have any questions or disagreement with your credit file

```
CREDIT REPORTING OFFICE          <===  Please address all  ===>   CREDIT REPORTING OFFICE
BUSINESS ADDRESS                        future correspondence      BUSINESS ADDRESS
CITY, STATE 00000                       to the address shown.      CITY, STATE 00000
PHONE NUMBER                                                       PHONE NUMBER

YOUR NAME                     DATE 05/10/96
123 HOME ADDRESS              SOCIAL SECURITY NUMBER 123-45-6789
CITY, STATE 00000             DATE OF BIRTH 04/19/57
```

CREDIT HISTORY

The first item identifies the business that is reporting the information.

This is your account number with the company reporting.

Number of months account payment history has been reported

This is the month and year you opened the account with the credit grantor.

See explanation below.

This is the date of last activity on the account and may be the date of last payment or the date of last change.

The highest amount charged or the credit limit.

Represents number of installments (M=Months) or monthly payments

The amount owed on the account at the time it was reported.

This figure indicates any amount past due at the time the information was reported.

Date of last account update.

(See explanation below.)

Credit History Section
List of both open and closed accounts.

Company Name	Account Number	Whose Acct.	Date Opened	Months Re-viewed	Date of Last Activity	High Credit	Terms	Items as of Date Reported			Date Reported
								Balance	Past Due	Status	
SEARS	11251514	J	05/86	66	05/96	3500		0		R1	05/96
AMOUNT IN H/C COLUMN IS CREDIT LIMIT											
CITIBANK	2953900000100473	I	11/86	48	05/96	9388	48M	0		I1	05/96
DINERS	355411251511	A	06/87	24	03/96	500		0		01	04/96
CLOSED ACCOUNT											
CHASE	54229778	I	05/85	48	12/95	5000	170	3000	680	R5	04/96

```
>>> PRIOR PAYING HISTORY - 30(03) 60(04) 90+(01) 01/96-R2, 02/96-R3, 03/96-R4 <<<
```

Number of times account was either 30/60/90 days past due

Date two most recent delinquencies occurred plus date of most severe delinquency

Collection Agency Accounts
Accounts which your creditors turned over to a collection agency.

```
>>> COLLECTION REPORTED 05/96; ASSIGNED 09/93 TO PRO COLL (800) XXX-XXXX
    CLIENT-ABC HOSPITAL; AMOUNT-$978; STAT UNPAID 05/96; BALANCE-$978 05/96
    DATE OF LAST ACTIVITY 09/93; INDIVIDUAL; ACCOUNT NUMBER 787652JC

>>>>>>>>>>>>>>>>>>> COLLECTION AGENCY TELEPHONE NUMBER(S) <<<<<<<<<<<<<<<<<<<
    PRO COLL (800) XXX-XXXX

    ******************PUBLIC RECORDS OR OTHER INFORMATION******************
```

Courthouse Records
Public Record items obtained from local, state and federal courts.

```
>>> LIEN FILED 03/93; FULTON CTY; CASE OR OTHER ID NUMBER-32114; AMOUNT-$26667;
    CLASS-STATE; RELEASED 07/93; VERIFIED 07/93

>>> BANKRUPTCY FILED 12/92; NORTHERN DIST CT; CASE OR OTHER ID NUMBER-673HC12;
    LIABILITIES-$15787; PERSONAL; INDIVIDUAL; DISCHARGED; ASSETS-$780

>>> JUDGMENT FILED 07/94; FULTON CTY; CASE OR OTHER ID NUMBER-898872; DEFENDANT-
    JOHN CONSUMER AMOUNT-$8984; PLANTIFF-ABC REAL ESTATE; SATISFIED 03/95; VERIFIED
    05/95
```

Additional Information
Primarily consists of former/other addresses and employments reported by your creditors.

```
    *******************ADDITIONAL INFORMATION*******************
    FORMER/OTHER ADDRESS 456 HOME RD, ATLANTA, GA 30000

    FORMER/OTHER ADDRESS P.O. BOX XXXX, SAVANNAH, GA 40000

    LAST REPORTED EMPLOYMENT - ENGINEER, SPACE PATROL

    *******COMPANIES THAT REQUESTED YOUR CREDIT HISTORY*************
```

Inquiry Section
List of businesses that have received your credit file in the last 24 months.

```
05/10/96  DISCLOSURE                    04/12/96  MACYS
03/16/96  PRM VISA                      02/01/96  AM CITIBANK
01/21/96  NATIONS BANK                  01/12/96  AR SEARS
05/17/95  JC PENNEY                     03/29/95  GE CAPITAL
```

THE FOLLOWING INQUIRIES ARE **NOT** REPORTED TO BUSINESSES:

PRM - This type of inquiry means that only your name and address were given to a credit grantor so they could offer you an application for credit. (PRM inquiries may remain for up to twelve months*.)

AM or **AR** - These inquiries indicate a periodic review of your credit history by one of your creditors. (AM and AR inquiries may remain for up to twelve months*.)

DISCLOSURE, ACIS or **UPDATE** - These inquiries indicate our activity in reponse to your contact with us for either a copy of your credit file or a request for research.

PRM, AM, AR, DISCLOSURE, ACIS and **UPDATE** inquiries do not show on credit files that businesses receive, only on copies provided to you.
*Twelve months for Connecticut residents.

WHOSE ACCOUNT

Indicates who is responsible for the account and the type of participation you have with the account.

J = Joint

I = Indiv...

Step 3. *Write the credit bureau.* According to the Federal Fair Credit Reporting Act, the credit bureau has to correct any errors on your file within a "reasonable time" after receiving your letter. The courts have deemed "reasonable" to be thirty days. You should send a separate letter for each inaccurate entry and *always* send them certified mail, return receipt requested. That way, when the receipt comes back, you can start counting. The letter on page 124 is a good model to use when writing the credit bureau to report inaccuracies.

After thirty days, you will have to follow up with the bureau by calling them—it's not likely they will call you. Most bureaus move slowly because they are overloaded. If they can't confirm the information on your report, firmly request that the entire entry be removed. You will likely have to assert yourself for the bureau to comply, but, as you do, remember Napoleon's words: "Victory belongs to the most persevering."

If the credit bureau refuses to cooperate, then contact the Federal Trade Commission (FTC) or your state consumer affairs department for help. (See the appendix, page 255 for the headquarters phone number and address.) The national credit bureaus report to the FTC and the local credit bureaus report to the state consumer affairs departments.

Keep in mind that many credit card companies and lenders use credit bureau databases to offer preapproved credit. In order not to receive preapproved offers, you can write to Equifax Options, P.O. Box 740123, Atlanta, Georgia 30374-0123. Include your complete name, full address, Social Security number, and signature. Equifax will remove your name from the lists they provide and will share your request with the other two national credit reporting agencies.

In order not to receive direct marketing mailings, write to Direct Marketing Association, Mail Preference Service, P.O. Box 9008, Farmingdale, New York 11735-9008. Again, include your complete name, full address, Social Security number, and signature. The DMA will remove your name from the mailing lists.

Whether you are struggling to manage collectors and creditors or cleaning

Sample Credit Bureau Letter

[Date] _____

From

_____

_____

_____

[To]

_____

_____

_____

RE: _____

Dear _____:

In reviewing the attached credit bureau report issued by your agency, I have detected an error regarding the following account.

    Company Name: _____

    Account Number: _____

Under the provision set forth in the 1977 Federal Fair Credit Reporting Act, I hereby request that your agency prove to me in writing the accuracy of the reporting of this account. Under the terms of the Act and succeeding court cases, you have 30 days to prove such accuracy or remove the account entirely from my report, and I ask that you do so.

You will note that this letter was sent certified mail, and that I expect a response within the said 30-day period. Should I not hear promptly from you, I *will* follow up with whatever action is necessary to cause my report to be corrected.

Please feel free to call me if you have any questions. My home phone number is _____ and my office number is _____.

Sincerely,

_____

up an inaccurate credit report, the key to your success is communication: Call the creditors more than they call you. Write to the credit bureau and send the letter return receipt requested. Follow up on letters and phone calls. Make sure you get what you request—a record that accurately reflects your credit history.

The Peace Track

Baby Step Checkup

Baby Step	Done	Action Needed to Complete	Date
1. Save $1,000 in an emergency fund.			
2. Pay off all debt but the mortgage with the debt snowball.			

If you are still paying off your debt, then it's likely you also need a credit checkup. When was the last time you saw your credit report?

_____

If you haven't checked your credit in the past two years, then make it one of your goals this week to call the credit bureau and order a copy of your report. It will cost from $3 to $15; free copies are available if you have been denied credit in the past sixty days and the creditor used their services. The national credit bureau numbers are listed in the appendix on page 255.

If you have received your credit report but have put off reporting inaccuracies, then set a date on your weekly goals chart to write letters notifying the bureau of the mistakes. Call your financial buddy and have him hold you accountable for completing the letter-writing exercise.

Weekly Goals

	Goal	Date
Spiritual		
Relational		
Physical		
Mental		

Part 3

Watch Your Wealth Grow

EIGHT

Show Me the Money: Make Compound Interest Work for You

NOW THAT YOU'VE LEARNED how to get out of and stay out of debt, we can focus on the real fun of personal finance: saving and building wealth so you can accomplish long-term goals, including funding your retirement or your children's college education, or paying off your house. There are at least three reasons you need to consistently save part of what you earn every week or month:

1. Emergencies
2. Major purchases, such as cars and furniture
3. Wealth building: giving, retirement, estate planning

As elementary as that may seem, few people save. Consider: America is one of the richest countries in the world, yet the average family has $1,000 or less in the bank.

According to a Department of Commerce, Bureau of Economics Analysis report, Americans save less of their income than anyone else in the world. The *National Accounts Statistics* states that Americans save less than 6 percent of their income, compared with people in West Germany, Japan, and South Korea, who save 12 percent to 28 percent of their income.

If you are serious about financial peace, then saving needs to become a way of life. In the next few pages, you will see what can happen when you create a disciplined savings program for yourself, as well as clarify what your short- and long-term savings goals are.

When you decide how much you want to put away, you may have to go back to your budget and revise it so you can afford to save more. On the other hand, if you strap yourself to a lifestyle you can't yet afford, it will prevent you from ever living well.

Take a few minutes now to think seriously about what is keeping you from saving.

_____

_____

_____

_____

What will make you save?

_____

_____

_____

It will be hard to make saving a way of life if you can't control your spending. That's why it's important for you to exercise bargain-hunting skills every time you shop.

What have you bought in the last week that you didn't need?

_____

_____

_____

What have you bought that you could have bought for less?

_____

_____

_____

Review the four steps to gaining power over purchase and the lucky seven principles of negotiation in chapter 6 before you head to the store again.

Wake-up Call! 🐓

The key to saving is sacrifice. You have to be willing to give up something now so you can have more later.

The Power of Compounding Interest

"What surprised me most about my credit card debt was how quickly it added up," Kit admitted one day. "One month I owed $500; then I paid the minimums for a couple of months. Suddenly, I owed $3,000. I guess that interest adds up faster than you think."

Kit had ignored a basic money principle, which we talked about in chapter 1: Money is active. While she and the girls were out spending and gaining short-term relief from the stress of the divorce, time and 17 percent interest rates were working on her credit card balance, increasing it exponentially. Kit had encountered the force of *compounding interest.*

Like Kit, most consumers don't understand the power of compounding interest to make or break you financially. When you save, time and interest rates work together to grow your money: Your dollars earn interest that earns interest on the interest, and so on. When you borrow, the compounding monster turns into your worst enemy.

How much do you pay each month toward retiring long-term debt (five or more years)?

_____

How much could you earn if you had that money free to save in a 12-percent-interest-bearing mutual account? To find out, look for the approximate monthly payment in the far left column of the "Pay Me Now or Pay Yourself" chart on page 132. Then look for the number of years it will take you to pay off that debt, at the top of the chart. The number listed equals the amount you could save. Say you have a five-year, $800-a-month banknote.

Pay Me Now or Pay Yourself

Years Invested Monthly at 12% Per Year

Monthly Payment	5	7	10	12	15	20	25	30	40
100	8,167	13,067	23,004	31,906	49,958	98,925	187,885	349,496	1,176,477
200	16,334	26,135	46,008	63,812	99,916	197,851	375,769	698,993	2,352,954
300	24,500	39,201	69,012	95,718	149,874	296,777	563,654	1,048,489	3,529,431
400	32,668	52,268	92,015	127,625	199,832	395,702	751,538	1,397,985	4,705,909
500	40,835	65,336	115,019	159,531	249,790	494,627	939,423	1,747,482	5,882,386
600	49,002	78,403	138,023	191,437	299,748	593,553	1,127,308	2,096,978	7,058,863
700	57,168	91,470	161,027	223,343	349,706	692,479	1,315,193	2,446,475	8,235,341
800	65,336	104,538	184,031	255,249	399,664	791,404	1,503,077	2,795,971	9,411,818
900	73,503	117,605	207,034	287,155	449,622	890,330	1,690,962	3,145,468	10,588,295
1000	81,669	130,672	230,039	319,061	499,580	989,255	1,878,847	3,494,964	11,764,772
1200	98,004	156,807	276,046	382,874	599,496	1,187,106	2,254,616	4,193,957	14,117,727
1500	122,504	196,008	345,058	494,545	749,370	1,483,883	2,818,270	5,242,446	17,647,159
2000	163,339	261,344	460,077	638,123	999,160	1,978,511	3,757,693	6,989,928	23,529,545

If you had that money free, you could, in five years, save $65,336 at 12 percent interest.

So what's it going to be? Are you going to make compounding interest your friend or your foe? Maybe the rest of the chapter will convince you. Let's look more closely at how compounding interest can work for you in two areas of savings: major purchases, or the sinking fund, and wealth building.

The Sinking Fund

The sinking fund is for high-ticket items, such as cars and furniture. Depending on how soon you need to buy one of those items, you can choose to start a sinking fund in a bank savings account or a mutual fund account. Either way, compound interest works for you in the sinking fund because it grows your money so you can pay cash for your purchases rather than borrow the money and then owe the cost of your purchase plus interest. Essentially, you make payments in reverse—*before* you buy the product and *to yourself,* or your account, instead of *after* you buy the product and *to a store or bank.*

For example, you may want a $4,000 dining-room suite. You can save $160 a month in a bank savings account for twenty-four months. That's only $3,840, but the interest on a 4-percent-interest-bearing account will yield the additional $160. (Mutual funds typically yield a higher rate of interest, but it's not a good idea to invest in a fund unless you plan to leave your money in for at least five years. For short-term goals—say one to three years—put your money in a money market account, which may yield as much as 5 to 6 percent, or a bank savings account, which yields around 4 or 5 percent.) If, instead of paying cash for your furniture, you choose to finance the suite at the store, you will likely be charged a 24 percent interest rate. That means you will pay more for your furniture and over a longer period of time than it took for you to save the cash to pay for it: $151 for thirty-one months for a total of $4,681.

Now let's move to a bigger-ticket item—the family car. Car payments can be the biggest waste of money! Who wouldn't love to drive paid-for cars for the rest of his life? The power of compounding interest can help.

J. G. and Jill bought a used car for $4,100 cash. Even though they won't need another car for a while, they decide to start saving for the next one right away. So they put $200 a month into a mutual fund at 10 percent interest. By year seven, they will likely need a new car, but they will be ready: Their savings will have grown to approximately $24,190. Now they can buy a new $16,000 car, have no monthly payments, and still have $8,190 in the bank.

After buying this new car, J. G. and Jill decide to continue saving for their next car, but they cut back their monthly payment to $100. At the end of seven more years, that $8,190 left over plus the $100-per-month investment grows to $28,540. Again, they have a seven-year-old car they want to dump for a new one. So they buy yet another $16,000 car for cash, leaving $12,539 in savings. For another seven years, they have no car payment, but they quit saving. Even so, the $12,540 at 10 percent will grow to $25,179.

The bottom line: By sacrificing with a lesser purchase up front and saving the difference, J. G. and Jill can drive paid-for cars and have savings the rest of their lives. That is compound interest working for you.

Wealth Building

Another area compound interest can work for you is wealth building. As little as $65 a month, saved in a mutual fund that yields an average of 12 percent interest a year, from age twenty to sixty-five, can grow to $1,394,555 for retirement.

How much your money can earn doesn't necessarily depend on how much you put in. Rather, your money's growth depends on the interest rates and how many years you save. Let's look at how the interest rates affect your savings first.

Say you make a onetime deposit of $1,000 into an exceptional money market account—6 percent—at age twenty-five and never deposit or withdraw from that account again until you reach age sixty-five. At 6 percent per year, your deposit grows to a little more than $10,000. If, however, you invest in a mutual fund (see chapter 9) that pays an average of 12 percent a year, your money will grow to $16,000, right? Wrong! You will have more than $93,000! If you can invest at 18 percent, you will have $750,378 at age sixty-five!

$1,000 onetime investment, no withdrawal, age 25 to age 65 (40 years)

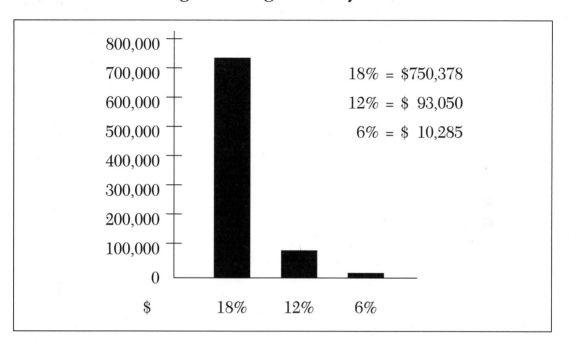

18% = $750,378

12% = $ 93,050

6% = $ 10,285

How long you save is also important. Bernard Zick, who has an M.B.A. and is an expert in the time value of money, gave this consumer quiz in his monthly newsletter, which demonstrates the power of compound interest and the importance of starting to save now:

Ben, age 22, invests $1,000 per year compounded annually at 10 percent for eight years until he is 30 years old. For the next 35 years, until he is 65, Ben invests not one penny more. Arthur age 30, invests $1,000 per year for 35 years until he is 65. His investment also earns 10 percent compounded annually. At age 65, will Arthur or Ben have the most money? The answer is in the chart on page 136.

10% Annual Compounding Interest

Age	Ben's Investment	Ben's Interest	Arthur's Investment	Arthur's Interest
22	1,000	1,100	0	0
23	1,000	2,310	0	0
24	1,000	3,641	0	0
25	1,000	5,105	0	0
26	1,000	6,716	0	0
27	1,000	8,487	0	0
28	1,000	10,436	0	0
29	1,000	12,579	0	0
30	0	13,837	1,000	1,100
31	0	15,221	1,000	2,310
32	0	16,743	1,000	3,641
33	0	18,418	1,000	5,105
34	0	20,259	1,000	6,716
35	0	22,285	1,000	8,487
36	0	24,514	1,000	10,436
37	0	26,965	1,000	12,579
38	0	29,662	1,000	14,937
39	0	32,628	1,000	17,531
40	0	35,891	1,000	20,384
41	0	39,480	1,000	23,523
42	0	43,428	1,000	26,975
43	0	47,771	1,000	30,772
44	0	52,548	1,000	34,950
45	0	57,802	1,000	39,545
46	0	63,583	1,000	44,599
47	0	69,941	1,000	50,159
48	0	76,935	1,000	56,275
49	0	84,628	1,000	63,002
50	0	93,091	1,000	70,403
51	0	102,400	1,000	78,543
52	0	112,640	1,000	87,497
53	0	123,904	1,000	97,347
54	0	136,295	1,000	108,182
55	0	149,924	1,000	120,100
56	0	164,917	1,000	133,210
57	0	181,409	1,000	147,631
58	0	199,549	1,000	163,494
59	0	219,504	1,000	180,943
60	0	241,455	1,000	200,138
61	0	265,600	1,000	221,252
62	0	292,160	1,000	244,477
63	0	321,376	1,000	270,024
64	0	353,514	1,000	298,127
65	0	388,865	1,000	329,039

Did you find the answer? Arthur never caught up!

There is no excuse for you not to retire a millionaire if you start saving while you are young and you save consistently at good interest rates.

Baby Step 3: Complete the Emergency Fund

It's time to befriend compound interest, to allow it to grow your money, by creating a savings plan. You can start by taking baby step 3:

Complete your emergency fund by saving three to six months' expenses.

You have already saved $1,000 for emergencies, but that won't be enough if you get laid off by your company, as Barry did, and have to spend three months looking for a new job.

Wake-up Call!

According to *Money* magazine, 75 percent of families will have a major financial setback in any ten-year period.

If Barry and Emily had had six months' living expenses in savings when he was first laid off, they never would have had to turn to their credit cards for help. Avoid a similar predicament, and take baby step 3. Complete your emergency fund. If you spend $36,000 a year, you should have $9,000 to $18,000 saved in a liquid account, such as a bank savings or a money market account on which you can write checks.

Beware certificates of deposit (CDs) and rental real estate: They are *not* liquid savings. You typically can't get money that's tied up in a CD without paying a stiff penalty for early withdrawal, and renters don't always pay. Also, keep in mind that the interest rates for liquid accounts are typically low, so don't expect compound interest to grow your savings by much. You will likely be dipping into your emergency fund too often for it to grow anyhow.

Take time to create an action plan to complete your emergency fund by the end of the year. Referring to your budget on page 74, figure out what three to six months' expenses add up to, and write that in the blank.

_____

Now, figure out how much you can save each month to complete the fund. Make a list of ways you can cut back on your spending and how much you will save. (Example: *Cancel magazine subscriptions; save $70 a year.*) Put that money toward your emergency fund.

Item to Cut	Amount Saved

You Work Hard for the Money: Create a General Savings Plan

After you have completed your emergency fund, it's time to start saving to meet short- and long-term goals. You work and slave at your job all your life, just to bring home the bacon and watch it walk right back out the door. Instead of getting ahead, your checkbook serves as a clearing account for the people you owe and the "stuff" you buy. You can stop that cycle by adding a new name to your list of bills: you.

There's a reason the "Savings" category comes second on the list of budget expenses. You are *supposed* to pay yourself before you pay any other bills. You need that money for your future. A great goal is 10 percent of your take-home pay, but even if you have to save less for a while, do it. It is ridiculous for you to spend your entire life at work only to end up broke and discouraged because you did not save every week.

You will stay motivated in your new commitment to save if you know what you are saving for. In the space provided, write your five-, ten-, and twenty-year savings goals.

Five-Year Goals

Example: *Redecorate the house*

1. _____
2. _____
3. _____
4. _____

Ten-Year Goals

Example: *Vacation in Europe*

1. _____
2. _____
3. _____
4. _____

Twenty-Year Goals

Example: *Children's college education*

1. _____
2. _____
3. _____
4. _____

In chapter 10, you will learn how to create a monthly savings plan for your retirement and your children's college education so those costs don't bankrupt you. For now, take time to create a savings plan for your five-year savings goals. In the short-term savings plan chart below, write what you are saving for, when you would like to buy it (that will tell you how long you have to save), and how much it will cost. (See chapter 6 for getting the best price.) If you can wait for at least five years before you make your purchase, you can save for the item in one of the many mutual funds available, of which 92 percent have averaged 12 percent annual growth over the last twenty years. Otherwise, you will need to save in a bank account, which yields 4 to 6 percent interest. Then figure out how much you need to save each month to earn enough interest so that by the time you want to make your purchase the savings and interest combined equal the purchase price. You will need to use a financial calculator, or you can ask your banker for help.

Short-Term Savings Plan

Item	Cost	Date to Purchase	Monthly Savings

Keep a copy of this chart where you can see it as a reminder to "show yourself the money."

Where Do You Save?

If you are not used to saving money or you just don't have the discipline yet, here are two methods that will help you get started:

1. *Forced savings plans.* If you have access to a credit union, you can set up a payroll deduction savings plan. The savings are deducted before you get your check, so that way you don't have a chance to do anything else with it. Most local banks also have forced savings programs. If you need to start this way, do it.

2. *PAC (Preauthorized Checking) withdrawal system.* Many insurance companies and security brokerage firms use PAC systems. Each month, a certain amount is automatically withdrawn from your checking account and deposited into a savings program, such as an annuity, a money market, or a mutual fund.

Attitude Check

As you save money and begin to build wealth, it's important to keep in mind these two principles:

1. Grow your wealth slowly.
2. Keep your attitude in check.

Most of our society defines a financial genius as someone who can make money faster than he can spend it. We have been misled. Financial geniuses know that the best way to get rich quick is to make wise decisions and let time—and compound interest—make you wealthy.

Then, as their cash increases, smart money managers keep their attitude in check. They realize that money is active even in the spiritual sense. So as their money grows, they continue to own it rather than allow it to own them. They aren't changed by wealth. They avoid increasing their lifestyle every time their income increases. Instead, they continue to save and invest as did the wise men described in Proverbs 21:20: "In the house of the wise are stores of choice food and oil, but a foolish man devours all he has."

After more than twenty years of studying the affluent, Drs. Thomas J. Stanley and William D. Danko described who becomes wealthy in their book *The Millionaire Next Door: The Surprising Secrets of America's Wealth*:

> Usually the wealthy individual is a businessman who has lived in the same town for all of his adult life. This person owns a small factory, a chain of stores, or a service company. He has married once and remains married. He lives next door to people with a fraction of his wealth. He is a compulsive saver and investor. And he has made his money on his own. *Eighty percent of America's millionaires are first-generation rich.*

By now you can see the power that managing your own money gives you; it allows you to control your finances rather than the other way around. If you will heed the power of compounding interest and make it work for you, you are ready to go from being in control to turning your dreams into a reality.

The Peace Track

Baby Step Checkup

It's important to get out of debt before you start saving for purchases or even before completing your emergency fund. If you haven't already paid off your debt, continue working on that. How many debts on the debt snowball have you paid off? How long will it take to pay off the next debt on the list? Don't

Baby Step	Done	Action Needed to Complete	Date
1. Save $1,000 in an emergency fund.			
2. Pay off all debt using the debt snowball.			
3. Complete your emergency fund by saving three to six months' expenses.			

give up. Instead, as you pay those bills, remember what football coach Vince Lombardi said: "The harder you work, the harder it is to surrender."

One way to keep your attitude in check as you build wealth is to have well-established priorities, to know what matters most to you so you aren't changed by money. In chapter 2, you named your top five priorities and kept a log to help you decide how your spending reflected your priorities. This week, take time to look back over that list (page 23) and to think about how your lifestyle reflects those. Would someone know what your priorities are just by watching you? Talk with a friend or your spouse about what and how you can change so you are living in a way that is consistent with what you say matters to you. Write your priorities on a separate sheet of paper and tape them to the mirror in your bathroom or someplace where you will see them every day. Make it a practice to review your priorities once a week and take time to evaluate how well you are living according to those.

Weekly Goals

	Goal	Date
Spiritual		
Relational		
Physical		
Mental		

Spread It Around:
The Power of Diversification

"C'MON, BARRY," Dennis insisted. "You really should consider investing in this one stock I'm telling you about. The company's earnings per share are low right now because the company just went through a major restructuring. But they've got this hot new product coming out next quarter, and I'm telling you, they are going to hit it big—really big."

Barry, Emily, and Dennis had stayed after the FPU seminar one evening and the talk had turned to stocks. Dennis had a hot tip on a stock from his stockbroker and had sold most of his friends on talking to his broker—except Barry.

"I don't know, Dennis," Barry said, hesitating. "I'd love to make some quick cash, but the stock market scares me. I don't really understand it all that well—what drives it up and down. Besides, we just put $5,000 into a six-month certificate of deposit."

Like Dennis and Barry, most people operate from one of two extremes when it comes to investing: unnecessary risk or stagnation. Typically, the riskier the investment, the higher the return; and conversely, the lower the risk, the lower the return. Investors call that the *risk-return ratio*.

If you put too much importance on an investment's potential returns without weighing the risk, you can lose everything. Dennis proved that. Two months prior to his conversation with Barry, he had admitted to his Financial Peace group that he had lost the $5,000 he had borrowed from his grandfather on an investment that had gone south. He still had $7,600 worth of stocks his grandfather had given him though.

On the other hand, playing it too safe can get you stuck, growing your money nowhere fast—like Barry. His investment ignorance kept him from being aggressive enough. He wanted guarantees, so he avoided stocks and instead purchased a $5,000 CD that paid a 4.2 percent return. The average inflation rate for the past seventy years has been 4 percent, which means Barry was earning about 0.2 percent on his investment per year. After taxes and inflation, Barry got his guarantee—a guaranteed loss, that is.

How can you get the best return on your money with the least amount of risk? Diversify. Spread your money among several investments so that your winners offset the negative results of the losers. We'll examine how you can begin using the power of diversification to grow your money. But first, let's dispel some common investing myths that may be hindering you from moving forward on the road to wild, wild wealth.

Investing Myths

Like many novice stock investors, Dennis had visions of dollar signs dancing in his head. As a result, he twice bought into a common investing myth—that you can get an immediate return on your investment. You can keep from losing your shirt by avoiding the following myths. Check the ones you have fallen prey to in the past.

___**Myth 1: Just because someone sells stock means he is a stock expert.** Wrong! Most insurance and investment people spend 80 percent of their time learning how to sell and 20 percent learning what to sell. Do not assume that just because someone has a license to sell investments he knows what he's doing or is the best person to handle your money.

___**Myth 2: My investment will grow overnight.** If something sounds too good to be true, it is. Proverbs 28:20 says, "He who hastens to be rich will not go unpunished." If the investment looks like a get-rich quick scheme, stay away from it!

___**Myth 3: "But it's a tax savings. . . ."** Tax deals are usually bad economic deals; that's why they have a tax benefit to them. There are tax credits on lower-income housing, for example; but lower-income housing tends to get torn up, which makes it a weak asset. If you're going to invest, *do it for the returns only.* If it turns out you can use the investment as a tax shelter, great. But consider that an *added* benefit and *not* the primary reason you invest.

___**Myth 4: It's okay to borrow to invest.** Don't even think about it! If the investment goes bad, you still have to pay back what you borrowed, plus interest. That means you would be losing more than you put into the investment to begin with.

___**Myth 5: The more sophisticated, the better the investment.** Puhlease! By now, you should know me well enough to know I would hate this idea. Instead rely on the KISS principle of investing: *Keep it simple, stupid!* Just because an investment looks and sounds sophisticated doesn't mean you are going to profit from it. Never put money in anything you don't understand.

In the space provided, write what happened when you bought into the myths you checked.

_____

_____

_____

_____

_____

By the time you finish reading this chapter, you will have the basic knowledge you need to make smart investment choices. Trust yourself—not the quality of suit selling you the "opportunity of a lifetime."

The Power of Diversification

Investments are like manure; they work better when you spread them around. That's what diversification does for you. It spreads out your investments, giving your money several places to grow. That way you decrease your risk; and in the end, you typically make more.

The graph on page 149 illustrates how diversification works for you. Two investors have $10,000. Investor 1 puts all of his money into a 7-percent-interest-bearing account for twenty-five years. Investor 2 diversifies. He puts $2,000 under his mattress and spreads the rest over four accounts that earn varying rates of return. He, too, leaves his money alone for the next twenty-five years.

By putting his money into a single account, the first investor's $10,000 grows to $54,274. The second investor's money, on the other hand, grows 77 percent more—to $96,280—because he spread his money around. He even lost $2,000 in a deal!

Wake-up Call!

If you have more than $15,000 in cash, it's time for you to diversify—and not just by investing. Consider saving your money in more than one bank. Banks can fail; and although Federal Deposit Insurance Corporation banks insure individuals up to $100,000, it can take months, even years, for the FDIC to pay.

Diversify with Mutual Funds

Mutual funds provide the kind of diversification and 10 to 15 percent returns that Investor 2 got on his money. For as little as $25 to $50 a month, or even $250 to $500 onetime investments, you can pool your money in a mutual fund with hundreds of other investors to buy and sell stocks.

Because there is more money in the fund to spend, you can afford to buy more stocks, which creates a hedge against risk. Plus, each fund has an expert manager who hires a team of stock analysts to do nothing but study the industries they have invested in for you. So if your stock fund invests in restaurants, a stock analyst who knows everything about the restaurant industry will work for that fund.

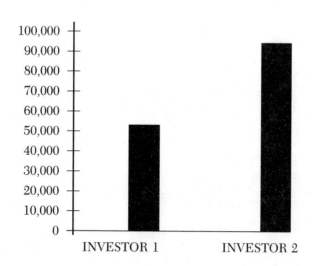

The Power of Diversification

Investor 1
Invests $10,000 for 25 years at 7%

Investor 2
Invests $2,000 and loses it all
Hides $2,000 under mattress
Invests $2,000 at 5% return
Invests $2,000 and gets a 10% return
Invests $2,000 and gets a 15% return
Leaves it alone for 25 years

**$54,274 without diversification; $96,280 with diversification
77% difference**

Why Not Single Stocks?

Why not invest in single stocks, the way Dennis did? For one, they are unpredictable. For every company that skyrockets from $5 to $105 a share in five to ten years, there are hundreds of publicly traded companies that go broke (can you say "Marvel Entertainment"?). What's more, the average investor—that's you and me—makes only a *7 percent return* on his single-stock investments. Don't believe it? Neither did Dennis.

Dennis insisted that his investments had outperformed the average Joe investor's during his four years out of school. So we put him through the following exercise. In the chart below, Dennis recorded the stocks he had invested in, along with the purchase price, the current price, and the gain or loss he had after owning the stock for four years. Then he multiplied the individual prices by 100 to get the total amount he invested, as well as the total gain.

Stock	Purchase Price	Current Price	Gain/Loss
Print Perfect	$ 19.00	$11.38	$ −7.62
Coffee Talk	$ 11.00	$34.00	$ 23.00
Sports Bag	$ 15.00	$17.63	$ 2.63
KidWorld	$ 25.00	$ 2.00	$−23.00
Entertain-Me Center	$ 6.00	$24.62	$ 18.62
TOTAL	$ 760.00	$89.63	$ 13.63
TOTAL × 100 shares	$7,600.00	$8,963	$ 1,363

The numbers are real but the stock names have been changed to protect the innocent and to avoid promoting any one particular stock.

To determine the percent increase in his portfolio, Dennis divided the net gain of $1,363 by the original investment, $7,600, and multiplied by 100:

$1,363 ÷ $7,600 = .17 × 100 = 17%
(Increase/ ÷ (Original = (% gain)
loss)　　　investment)

He then divided the net increase by the number of years his stocks had been invested:

17% ÷ 4 = 4.25%
(Net gain) ÷ (# of years) = (Average yield)

Dennis's investments grew 17 percent over four years, an average of 4.25 percent per year. That's *less* than the 7 percent per year average. Ouch!

If you own individual stocks, you can try the same exercise using the following chart and formulas.

Stock	Purchase Price	Current Price	Gain/Loss
TOTAL × number of shares			

Determine the total percent gain:

$$\underline{\hspace{2cm}} \div \underline{\hspace{2cm}} = \underline{\hspace{1.5cm}} \times \ 100 \ = \underline{\hspace{2cm}}$$

(Increase/   ÷   (Original   =   (% gain)
loss)   investment)

The average increase per year:

$$\underline{\hspace{2cm}} \div \underline{\hspace{2cm}} = \underline{\hspace{2.5cm}}$$

(Net gain)   ÷   (# of years)   (Average yield)

Wake-up Call!

Unless you earn $200,000-plus per year, you don't need to be taking big risks by buying individual stocks. That's because you can't afford to invest in enough stocks to offset poor returns.

If you don't research stocks for a living, you cannot hope to follow the necessary trends and measurements to pick stocks accurately. And even then, the pros don't always pick them right. Ever seen the *Wall Street Journal* dartboard contests? Professional stockbrokers pit their skills against a random stock selection to see whose picks pay off the highest returns. According to one 1996 *Wall Street Journal* report, the *darts* won 45 percent of the time—seventeen contests out of thirty-seven.

Why Not CDs and Money Markets?

Investing in mutual funds makes sense for another reason. There are two types of investment risks: 1) the risk of loss of principal, or the money you invest; and 2) the risk that inflation will beat you to the bank and take your money. Most people, including Barry, forget about inflation when they put their money in a bank savings account, CD, or money market.

Barry's CD is earning a safe 4.76 percent. Yet, for the past sixty years, inflation has averaged 4.07 percent per year. That means he is earning about 0.69 percent on his $5,000 investment. Even with inflation dipping to 2.7 percent as it did in 1996, a 4.76 percent certificate of depression—commonly known as a certificate of deposit—isn't going to grow your money very quickly. (Remember, the average mutual fund has yielded 12 percent a year.)

About the only good reason to put money in a bank savings account, CD, or money market fund: so you can save an emergency fund. The rate of return on an emergency fund isn't important. What *is* important is that you can get to it quickly (it needs to be a liquid account) and that it's a risk-free investment.

Create an Investment Strategy

If you have saved three to six months' expenses in an emergency fund, you are ready to create your own investment strategy. Although we will talk specifically about how you can save for retirement and college in the next chapter, you can use the space here to begin deciding what kinds of funds you feel comfortable investing in.

If you have more than $10,000 to invest (in addition to your emergency fund), you should try to spread your money over four of the following fund types—25 percent in each fund—according to how aggressive you want to be.

- **Balanced fund:** A calm fund that offers slow, steady growth—no big fluctuations in price or value. Investments include a balance of medium-sized company stocks for growth; stocks of large companies that don't grow much but pay dividends one to four times a year; and bonds.
- **Growth and income fund:** The first-time investor's friend because it is also relatively calm. This fund includes stocks of medium-sized, growing companies, as well as large, dividend-paying companies (hence, "growth" and "income").
- **Growth fund:** A more volatile fund that focuses on long-term growth,

the growth fund primarily includes medium-sized company stocks, with only a few of the larger companies represented.

- **International fund:** The more frequent ups and downs in this fund scare some people; but in the long run, the returns exceed those of a balanced fund. What's more, overseas stocks often perform well in the years U.S. companies don't, which makes investing at least part of your portfolio in an international fund a smart move.

- **Aggressive growth fund:** The most volatile of the funds, the aggressive growth fund buys smaller, more aggressive company stocks. So it either makes it big or busts, but don't be put off by the risk. Quality aggressive growth funds can yield as high as a 19 to 24 percent return. The trick is you may have to hold on for as long as ten years to see that kind of growth.

Use the space provided to list the funds you'd like to invest in. If you like an aggressive approach, for example, your long-term investment distribution might look like this:

25%	Growth and income
25%	Growth
25%	International fund
25%	Aggressive growth

Investors with more than $50,000 will want to find two or three funds of each type.

Your Long-Term Investment Distribution

_____

_____

_____

_____

Warning: Some people suggest investing in aggressive funds when you're young and then switching to calm, conservative funds when you retire. That's hogwash! "But everybody's doin' it that way, Dave!" Well, if you really want to follow the rest of the lemmings off the edge of the cliff, then go ahead.

Called asset allocation, changing your investment approach according to your age is a bad idea. People who depend on it typically invest too aggressively when they're young and not aggressively enough when they are old. Think about it: If you are sixty-five years old, you may live to be ninety-five. You still have thirty years you need to outpace inflation with some fairly aggressive growth.

Anyone who can afford to tie up his or her money for more than five years should do it in the four types of mutual funds discussed.

How to Choose the Best Fund

"Mutual funds sound like a great idea, Dave," Barry admitted, "but there are more than 5,000 funds out there. How do you narrow your choices and pick one?"

First, get a list of funds. A good place to look is in *Kiplinger's Personal Finance Magazine*. Beware of other sources; the editorial opinions can be skewed by advertisers. *Kiplinger's* typically lists the funds' 800-numbers, which you can call for sales materials on the funds that interest you.

There are four criteria you can use to help you evaluate a fund: performance, family, fluctuation, and expenses. The first two criteria should be given most importance when deciding where to invest.

1. Performance

A mutual fund's track record is the most important criterion you can use to help you decide whether to invest your money in it. Look for the average annual return over a five-year period. Don't buy baby funds. If the fund is only three years old, it still needs diapers. You want one that is old enough to have seen some hard times. How did the fund do after Black October 1987, for example? If the fund has at least a 10 to 15 percent average return over ten to fifteen years, including October '87, you have a good fund. Make sure when you compare track records or rates of return that you are comparing similar fund types. Compare a balanced fund to a balanced fund, for example.

2. *Family*

The next criterion to consider is the family of funds. Look for families that have been around ten years or more and that have performed well overall. Also find out whether the fund is managed by one person or a team of people. For years, most funds were managed by just one person. Peter Lynch, for example, was one of the best-known, most successful fund managers in the country. When he retired, however, the fund suffered. With team management, a fund is less likely to suffer when one person leaves. Diversification of management is as important as diversification of stocks.

3. *Fluctuation*

Not as important as the first two criteria, this is what I call the roller-coaster test. When you compare the same kinds of funds, it's important to see how much the fund fluctuates in value—that is, how much it rises and how low it dips. The statistic used to measure this roller-coaster ride is called the "beta," and can be found in the funds' sales materials. A beta of 1.0 is the exact "wildness," or fluctuation of the top five hundred stocks on the market, better known as the Standard & Poor's Index. A beta that is higher than 1.0 is more of a roller-coaster ride than the rest of the market. For aggressive growth funds, you should look for betas of 1.5 or 1.7. If your fund's beta is less than 1.0, then it is calmer than the overall stock market. Most balanced and growth-and-income funds, for example, have betas of approximately 0.9 or 0.8.

4. *Expenses*

The most overworked, overrated criterion for choosing a mutual fund is expenses. That's why I put it last on the list. In fact, forget the expense *ratio*. Instead, look for a simple chart in your fund's paperwork—the "prospectus"—for a "fee table" or "expense summary." That shows the average expenses investors pay per thousand dollars invested. The expenses over ten years, for example, may be $119. That's an average of $11.90 a year, or $1.19 per $1,000 invested.

No matter what the expenses turn out to be, keep in mind they should be your lowest priority on your list of criteria for choosing a fund. Fund A's expenses may be 0.5 percent higher than Fund B's, but Fund A has a 16 percent average return over ten years compared with Fund B's 9 percent average over the same time. Which would you choose?

One More Thing: Load Versus No-Load

Load funds pay commissions to the fund managers; no-loads don't. People frequently assume that the noncommission funds are cheaper or better, but don't be tricked. Some no-load funds have higher expenses than the ones that include commissions. There is no research showing one fund does better than another. Either type of fund makes a good investment.

Narrow It Down

After you decide on a long-term investment distribution and get a list of funds, it's time to use the four criteria to narrow your choices and select at least one fund of each type in your plan. You can use the chart on page 158 to record your findings as you research each fund and to help you make your decision.

Remember, *Kiplinger's Personal Finance Magazine* is a good resource for names of funds. A good stockbroker can also help you find the names of several funds that match the objectives of your investment distribution plan. When you are looking for a stockbroker or financial planner, take these three steps:

1. *Interview several to see whom you feel most comfortable with.* A broker or financial planner should have the heart of a teacher, not the heart of a salesman. Look for a personality match—someone you feel comfortable asking questions and who will encourage you to understand the process rather than ignore your questions.
2. *Check references.* Try to get a recommendation from a friend or relative.
3. *Ask whether the broker or planner receives a fee from the sale of any product, such as the investments or insurance.* If he does, there is a

Fund Name	Average % Return 10–15 Years	Fund Family Notes	Beta	Expenses
Growth & Income				
Growth				
International				
Aggressive Growth				

conflict of interest. That's not to say you can't get good advice from someone who receives a commission. But beware of his vested interest.

Other Investments to Know About

Mutual funds aren't the only kinds of investments available; they are about the only kind I recommend. There are, however, two types of investments you need to be aware of.

Bonds

People often think of bonds as being safer than stocks; but, in fact, they carry the same inherent problems and risks as stocks—namely, they don't offer the diversification mutual funds do. The difference in stocks and bonds: When you buy a stock, you buy a piece of ownership in a company. When you buy a bond, you are a creditor rather than an owner; essentially, you receive an IOU for a loan you make to the company.

Wake-up Call!

Just because the federal government guarantees Government National Mortgage Association (GNMA) and Federal National Mortgage Association (FNMA) bonds against default doesn't mean that the principal you invest in these bonds is guaranteed. It's not.

Many retirees invest in municipal bonds, which are bonds issued by cities and states, because the interest has no federal income tax on it. So you get more for your money. For example, if you are in a 30 percent income bracket, a municipal bond that pays 5 percent becomes the equivalent of a CD or taxable bond that pays 7.14 percent. The best way to invest in municipal bonds is through a municipal bond mutual fund.

Annuities

People frequently save for their retirement with annuities, which are savings accounts through insurance companies. Annuities pay more than banks do on savings accounts. Unlike banks, however, insurance companies are not protected by the FDIC; so your investment is only as safe as the insurance company is financially healthy.

If you have maxed out your pretax savings, which we will talk about in the next chapter, you may want to think about investing in a *variable annuity,* which is a mutual fund inside an annuity. The benefit: It allows your money to grow tax-deferred.

A Word About Real Estate

Other than mutual funds, real estate is one of my favorite investments. It can be a great hedge against inflation and a good vehicle for amassing wealth because of the tax benefits and cash flow that can be generated from the property. The problem with real estate as an investment: Rental property is the least liquid investment you can make (it's the hardest to get your cash back out of), so it carries a high degree of risk, particularly if you have no cash reserves.

One couple I counseled, for example, wanted to purchase a duplex so they could live in one side and rent the other. They figured that by paying half the mortgage themselves and charging the renters more than half of the mortgage, they could create extra income and eventually save enough for a down payment on another house. Sounds smart, right? Not exactly. The couple had debt and only a small savings account, so their plan actually threatened to send them deeper into debt. Even though they would have a "positive cash flow" on the house, meaning they would be taking in more rent than they were paying on the mortgage, major repairs on the house or a month without tenants would create a significant financial setback for them.

Before you invest in real estate, you should be able to check off every item in the following checklist:

_____You already own your own home.

_____You have *more* than three to six months' expenses saved.

_____You can pay cash or you are getting a deep, deep discount for the house.

Keep in mind: Most novice real estate investors pay way too much for properties. What's more, they borrow to do it. If your mortgage is $750 and you are charging $800 rent, you are setting yourself up to lose money. Tenants who fail to pay, vacancies, and the cost of maintenance can sink you. Your wealth-building scheme will soon turn into a white elephant you can't sell because you owe so much on the house. Look for deep discounts; then, borrow little or nothing on the house you plan to use as your rental property.

A lot of excitement is generated among the people who attend Financial Peace University when they start to pay off debt and see how the compounding interest and diversification can work for them. They gain a new sense of hope, which motivates them to cut back even more on their spending and find new ways to save. They feel the weight of financial anxiety lift from their shoulders and even increase their productivity. How about you? Are you starting to gain a sense of financial freedom?

The Peace Track

Record how far you have come taking the financial baby steps in the chart on page 162.

As you start to regain your sense of hope about your money, keep in mind that saving and investing wisely may give you financial peace, but there is another kind of peace money can't provide: the peace of mind and heart that comes from having a relationship with God and from living in a way that reflects His character—His truth, goodness, and compassion. You can work hard and save loads of money, but if you don't have God in your life, you will still have a void in your soul that causes you to wake up one day and ask, "Is this all there is?" Take time this week to read and think about Proverbs 15:16:

> Better is a little with the fear of the Lord,
> Than great treasure with trouble.

Baby Step Checkup

Baby Step	Done	Action Needed to Complete	Date
1. Save $1,000 in an emergency fund.			
2. Pay off all debt using the debt snowball.			
3. Complete your emergency fund by saving three to six months' expenses.			

Weekly Goals

	Goal	Date
Spiritual		
Relational		
Physical		
Mental		

TEN

To Everything There Is a Season: College and Retirement Planning

NOW THAT YOU HAVE a basic understanding of investments, it's time to put some of that knowledge to use. As we mentioned in the last chapter, investing is a great way to build wealth so you can achieve your long-term goals. For Barry and Emily, in their late thirties, and Kit, well into her forties, building a retirement fund was a particularly pressing issue. Barry and Emily had the added desire to save for their twelve-year-old son's college education.

According to a Gallup and Robinson survey quoted in *USA Today*, 80 percent of parents perceive college to be either indispensable or very valuable to their child's economic well-being, and 31 percent consider it their number-one financial priority. The parents are right: College gives you an advantage in the kind of job you are able to get; however, it is *not* a necessity. If it comes down to your choosing between saving for your kids' college education and saving for your own retirement, *choose your retirement.*

According to *Forbes* magazine, by 1993 more than sixty thousand American companies had eliminated their traditional pension plans, to which employees contributed nothing but from which they received their retirement. That means it is now up to you, the employees, to start saving for your own retirement. As a whole, Americans aren't doing this very well; a May 1995 *USA Today* article reported that only 44 percent of Americans are taking the hint and saving. I guess the other 56 percent are depending on what I call Social Insecurity.

A December 30, 1996, *USA Today* article reported that, in 2029, just as the last of the baby boomers turn sixty-five, Social Security will have *only* 77 percent of the money it needs to pay benefits. What's more, the U.S. Census Bureau states that 62 percent of Americans retire on less than $10,000 a year. It's time to take responsibility for your future.

You can get over the guilt trip about not paying your kids' way through college. In their book *The Millionaire Next Door*, Dr. Thomas Stanley and Dr. William Danko note that most millionaires in this country put themselves through school. It's not going to kill your kids to have to work to pay for their education. In fact, they may even profit from the experience. If you really want to help, save so you can eat and pay your bills during your retirement and start looking for scholarships for your kids. They will thank you when they can start their adult lives, debt-free and at peace knowing you are taken care of.

The Steps to Retirement Planning

Barry, Emily, and Kit felt the shadow of time slowly stretching over their heads and knew they needed to make retirement saving a priority. For Barry and Emily debt and poor planning had prevented them from putting anything aside. For Kit, it was the untimely divorce that had left her forty-three years old and without retirement savings.

J. G., Jill, and Dennis didn't feel the same pressure. "Retirement?" J. G. said quizzically when the issue came up one day. "Jill and I are too young to know how much we should save for retirement. I figure we'll just put aside what we can. We can get more disciplined about it later. Right now, we need to worry about saving for a house." Dennis reflected another common philosophy: Still convinced he would strike it rich before he turned thirty, he was more concerned with putting money into his new business than he was with a retirement plan. Remember Ben and Arthur in chapter 8? You can put off saving for your retirement but you will never catch up to the guy who started saving early.

Fortune magazine says that almost 75 percent of Americans fear they aren't saving enough for retirement. I have seen the panic-stricken faces of the people *Fortune* is talking about. They are fifty and sixty years old and thought Social Security would take care of them. Now, they can barely make it day to day. Don't make the same mistake. Instead, take these three steps to retirement planning:

1. *Set goals for your retirement.* Think about how you want to live during your retirement years—dream a little.
2. *Count the cost.* Calculate approximately how much it will take to fund your retirement lifestyle, and set a financial goal that will help you make that dream come true.
3. *Create a monthly savings program.* Choose the right investments to achieve your financial goal.

Let's take a look at each step more closely.

Step 1: Set Goals for Your Retirement

Before you decide what you want your annual retirement income to be, it's important to consider what kind of life you want to live during your twilight years. For example, some people plan to work until they reach seventy-five or eighty. Others want to quit at sixty-five and go back to college, just for the fun of it. One successful physician retired and then went to divinity school to study theology; he had always been interested in the subject, and now he finally had the time to do something about it.

The following exercise will help you take time to dream a little. Fill in the blanks as you imagine the day-to-day lifestyle you would like during retirement.

How old would you like to be when you retire?_____

How would you like to spend your time? Is there anything you can't do now that you would like to be able to do then? (*Example: Eat out more frequently; travel with grandchildren; paint or write a book; take a class; play golf; vacation with spouse.*)

_____
_____
_____
_____

Where would you like to live? In the house where you are now? Or would you like to build that dream house on the beach?

_____
_____

What would happen if you had to move into a nursing home or a retirement community? Have you visited any in your area? What are the facilities like? How much would it cost to live there?

_____
_____
_____
_____

Don't go and get depressed on me just because I mentioned "nursing home." I know, you may not want to think about it, but that isn't going to change if you eventually need full-time care. Better to think about it and plan for it now than to leave it to your children to pay for your nursing care. If you want to grow old comfortably and with dignity, you need to think about these things now.

Step 2: Count the Cost

Once you have a picture in your mind of your dream retirement, it's time to calculate how much you will need to fund the dream. Start by creating a sample retirement cash-flow plan. First, tally the current monthly expenses that will decrease or disappear after retirement. Your clothing budget, for example, should drop significantly when you quit working. After all, you won't have to buy new suits and dresses to maintain that professional image anymore. That should also help your dry-cleaning bills. Here is a list of expenses from your budget that will likely decrease at retirement:

- College savings fund
- Mortgage (if you have a fifteen-year mortgage, you will likely pay off your house by the time you retire)
- Clothing: children, adults, cleaning
- Child care
- Baby-sitter
- School tuition (unless you plan to help pay for your grandchildren's education)
- School supplies
- Child support (most retired parents' children are grown)
- Bank loans and credit card debts

Using their budget in chapter 4, pages 68–72, Barry and Emily made a list of expenses that would decrease by the amounts entered on page 168.

Note that Barry and Emily anticipated paying off their house and all other debts before retirement. They could eliminate child-related expenses—no children's clothing budget, no school supplies, no baby-sitter fees. Barry would no longer have professional organization dues to pay each month. The couple also decided they could cut back on their own clothing and dry-cleaning budgets. They currently pay $150 a month for clothing and $65 for dry cleaning (see page 70). During retirement, they plan on paying at least $30 a month less for clothing and $35 a month less for dry cleaning.

Another large expense Barry and Emily anticipated cutting back was their life insurance. Their ultimate goal for retirement was to become self-insured—that is, they planned to save enough so that if one of them died, they would have enough saved so that the other could make it without working

Housing

Mortgage	$1,132	
Subtotal		$1,132

Clothing

Children	$ 75	
Adults	$ 30	
Cleaning	$ 35	
Subtotal		$ 140

Personal

Life Insurance	$ 70	
Baby-sitter	$ 40	
School Supplies	$ 100	
Organization Dues	$ 25	
Subtotal		$ 235

Debts

Visa	$ 24	
MasterCard	$ 148	
Bank Loan	$ 567	
Subtotal		$ 739
TOTAL		$2,246

and without insurance income. If you have no debt, no kids at home, and somewhere between $500,000 and $700,000 in cash and mutual funds saved and you die, could your spouse struggle through?

Take time now to figure out how much the expenses from your monthly cash-flow plan on page 74 will decrease during your retirement. Note that only the expenses that are likely to decrease are listed on the worksheet on pages 169–70. If you do not anticipate an expense going down, leave the space blank.

Anticipated Reductions in Living Expenses

Saving
College Fund _____

Housing
First Mortgage _____
Second Mortgage _____
Replace Furniture _____
Subtotal _____

Clothing
Children _____
Adults _____
Cleaning _____
Subtotal _____

Personal
Life Insurance _____
Child Care _____
Baby-sitter _____
School Tuition _____
School Supplies _____
Child Support _____
Alimony _____
Organization Dues _____
Other _____
Other _____
Subtotal _____

Debts
Visa 1 _____
Visa 2 _____
MasterCard 1 _____
MasterCard 2 _____
American Express _____
Discover Card _____
Gas Card 1 _____

Continued on page 170

Debts (*cont.*)
Gas Card 2 _____
Dept. Store Card 1 _____
Dept. Store Card 2 _____
Finance Co. 1 _____
Finance Co. 2 _____
Credit Line _____
Student Loan 1 _____
Student Loan 2 _____
Other _____
Other _____
Subtotal _____
TOTAL _____

Hold on to this figure. You will use it in another formula.

Just as some expenses will decrease during retirement, others, including medical bills and the cost of life insurance, will increase. So you need to tally the expenses likely to go up. Barry and Emily's list of potentially increased expenses included the following:

Medical/Health
Doctor Bills | $100 |
Drugs | $ 50 |
Subtotal | | $150
Recreation
Vacation | $300 |
Subtotal | | $300
TOTAL | | $450

Note that Barry and Emily anticipated paying about $100 a month in doctor bills. That's 20 percent more than the $80 they now budgeted for their family of five (see page 70). Although their health care would likely cover whatever medical bills they might encounter during their senior years, they wanted to be prepared, so they decided to pad their estimated medical spending. They did the same with their estimated drug costs by increasing the figure from the current $10 (see page 70) to $50.

Also, their retirement dream included taking one big trip a year, as well as visiting their children wherever they lived. By looking at old vacation bills, they were able to estimate they might spend about $3,600 a year on travel. So they decided to plan on spending about $300 a month on vacations or saving for vacations during retirement.

Estimate the increased spending you may do during retirement:

Anticipated Increases in Living Expenses

Medical/Health
 Doctor Bills   _____
 Drugs   _____
 Subtotal   _____
Recreation
 Entertainment   _____
 Vacation   _____
Subtotal   _____
TOTAL   _____

Now, calculate your total estimated monthly living expenses. Find your current monthly living expenses from the cash-flow plan on page 74. Subtract your anticipated reductions from your current expenses. Then add your anticipated increases to that figure. Here's what Barry and Emily's math looked like:

$$\$5,174 - \$2,216 = \$2,928 + \$450 = \$3,378$$

Their annual expenses, or income needs, then would be:

$$\$3,378 \times 12 = \$40,536$$

Although Barry and Emily's anticipated expenses were about $40,000, they decided to save so they would have $45,000 a year income. The additional $5,000 gave them what they called a "just in case" padding and extra income to use to support financially one or two youth organizations they currently worked with. You can do the same—save extra for your retirement, that is. You don't have to limit yourself to saving only for your anticipated needs. Save as much as you can. Just make sure you can still meet your current monthly expenses.

Now fill in the blanks in the following formula using the total reductions (page 169) and increases (page 171) you anticipate to occur in your monthly expenses during retirement to get your estimated monthly retirement living expenses:

_____	− _____	= _____	+ _____	= _____
Current Expenses	Anticipated Reductions	Subtotal	Anticipated Increases	Monthly Total

_____	12	= _____
Monthly Total ×	12	= Annual Expenses

Unless you are clairvoyant, it's hard to plan for everything that might happen. No parent plans on raising his or her grandchild, for example, but more and more grandparents are taking on that responsibility today. That's why it's important for you to save as much as you can for retirement—not just what you will need.

Rather than go through the above exercise, Kit realized that once her children were grown, she could easily live as a single woman on her current $35,000 income. So she made that her retirement savings goal. On the other hand, J. G. and Jill thought they could retire on less than their $50,000 income but they didn't want to take any chances. So, like Kit, they simply decided to make their income their retirement goal.

Step 3: Create a Monthly Savings Program

How you determine what to put away monthly can be tricky. After all, inflation eats 2 to 4 percent of your savings each year. There is, however, a simple two-step formula that accounts for inflation while it helps you determine what to save each month. Here's how it worked for Barry and Emily.

1. *Determine the nest egg.* Barry and Emily wanted to save so they would have an annual retirement income of $45,000 in today's dollars. If they saved in a mutual fund at 12 percent per year, they would net about 8 percent annually because of inflation. So they divided their desired income by .08, for a total nest egg of $562,500.

$45,000	÷	.08	=	$562,500
Annual Desired Income	÷	Interest (Minus Inflation)	=	Nest Egg Needed

2. *Calculate the monthly savings.* Now they targeted their nest egg using an 8 percent accounting factor, appropriate to their age. (See the 8 percent factor table on page 174.) Because they were thirty-seven and thirty-eight years old, they used the factor for a forty-year-old and multiplied that by the nest egg to give them the monthly savings needed.

$562,500	×	.001051	=	$591.19
Nest Egg Needed	×	40-year-old Factor	=	Monthly Savings

Using the factor table on page 174, determine how much you need to save monthly for your retirement.

_____	÷	_____	=	_____
Annual Desired Income	÷	Interest (Minus Inflation)	=	Nest Egg Needed

8 Percent Inflation Factors

Age	Years to Save	Factor
25	40	.000286
30	35	.000436
35	30	.000671
40	25	.001051
45	20	.001698
50	15	.002890
55	10	.005466
60	5	.013610

Target your nest egg using the 8 percent factor for your age.

$$\underline{\hspace{3cm}} \times \underline{\hspace{3cm}} = \underline{\hspace{3cm}}$$

Nest Egg Needed × 40-year-old Factor = Monthly Savings

Almost $600 may sound like a lot to save every month, but the government has set up pretax savings programs that can help you accomplish your retirement goals. We'll talk about those programs next, but keep in mind that the earlier you start saving, the easier it will be on your monthly budget. Sadly, for Kit, she didn't have a choice but to start saving later in life.

Kit couldn't know she was going to be divorced at forty; otherwise, she could have worked and started her own retirement savings program when she was in her twenties. Instead, she wound up in her early forties with only seventeen years to save for retirement. (She wanted to retire at sixty.) Here is what her math looked like:

$$\$35,000 \div .08 = \$437,500$$
$$\$437,500 \times .002890 = \$1,264.38$$

After she paid her monthly expenses—the $640 mortgage on her house, the girls' clothing, etc.—she didn't have enough left over to save $1,264.38 a month. Working until age sixty-five, however, she would have to save only $742.88 a month, a more manageable goal, once she completed her emergency fund.

How Do You Save for the Dream? Baby Step 4

Knowing how much you need to save isn't enough. It's also important to know the best way to save. In chapter 8, you saw that mutual funds provide the best return on your investment over the long haul. Another key to saving and wealth building: Invest pretax dollars. Don't pay taxes on your money until you use it, billionaire J. Paul Getty advised. But how can you legally avoid taxes? Well, the government has created several tax-deferred compensation plans to help individuals save for retirement. The beauty of these plans: Say Barry and Emily, who are in a 30 percent income tax bracket, decide to save $6,700 a year for their retirement (about $558 a month). The tax on that amount is $2,000, which means they only have $4,700 to invest after they pay their taxes. Through a qualified retirement plan, however, the government allows Barry and Emily to keep their extra $2,000 a year, on one condition: At the end of the thirty-five years, they have to pay back the taxes. Invested at 12 percent for thirty-five years, the $2,000 that would have been taxed grows to $1,071,828. The whole $6,700 annual savings will grow to $3,590,619. Wow! Now that's a deal!

There are several specific kinds of pretax retirement funds you can contribute to.

Individual Retirement Account (IRA)

This is not a product sold at banks but a particular type of investment. A single person, like Kit, can invest $2,000 a year in an IRA, as long as she earns more than that amount, without paying taxes on the principal or the earnings until she withdraws it at retirement. In fact, the amount you put into your IRA can be tax deductible, under certain circumstances. Two-income families and married couples with one full-time homemaker can invest up to $4,000 a year if they earn more than that amount. That's a breakthrough for homemakers who, prior to 1997, were allowed to contribute only $250 a year to the IRA.

The 1997 tax-act changes allow an after-tax IRA, called the Roth IRA (for the senator who authored that portion of the bill). Married couples filing jointly with annual incomes below $150,000 and singles with incomes below $95,000 may contribute to a Roth IRA in addition to their company retirement plans. Although the Roth is an after-tax investment, it grows tax free! To be tax free, this IRA must not be taken out before you turn 59½ years old and must have been invested for five years.

One of the primary benefits of the Roth: After five years, you can withdraw money without tax or penalty for several reasons:

- You can withdraw up to $10,000 from the Roth to buy your first home.
- You can make a withdrawal to help pay for education.
- You can withdraw from your contributions—*not the growth*—to help you survive a major financial crisis that drains your emergency fund.

So, unlike the traditional IRA or 401(k) plan, which does penalize for early withdrawals, the Roth IRA offers a lot of flexibility, and it grows tax free.

401(k), 403(b), and 457 Plans

These are pretax savings plans the Internal Revenue Service allows corporations, nonprofit organizations, such as hospitals and school systems, and government organizations, such as utilities companies, to offer their employees. The 401(k) allows corporate employees to invest anywhere from 3 to 25 percent of their pretax income. Similarly, the 403(b) is offered by nonprofit organizations and the 457 is offered by government organizations. Some companies match employee investments by as much as 25 percent; but even if they don't, you should take advantage of the tax savings by contributing to your 401(k). It's dumb not to!

Simplified Employee Pension Plan (SEPP)

If you are self-employed like Dennis you can deduct up to 13.04 percent of your net profits before taxes each year and contribute them to a SEPP account. Small business owners can contribute up to $22,500 or 15 percent of their employees' compensation, whichever is less, to a SEPP each year.

Each of the above plans provides several investment options, including guaranteed investment contracts, or bonds, and mutual funds. For all the reasons we talked about in the last chapter—diversification, returns, and expert management—mutual funds are your best choice. Unless you are putting every penny you earn into paying off debt, there is no good reason for you not to invest in a qualified retirement plan. You can use all the tax savings you can get. So go ahead. Take baby step 4:

Invest 15 percent of your gross household income into Roth IRAs and pretax retirement plans.

Let's make and execute plans to retire with dignity. You should begin to invest 15 percent of your gross household income into retirement plans. Which plan do you choose?

Simple: If your employer matches a portion of your 401(k) (or other retirement plan) savings, then save enough in that account to get all the match. Then, if you are a couple who makes less than $150,000 a year or a single who makes less than $95,000 a year, you should fully fund a Roth IRA. That means you will contribute $2,000 ($4,000 for couples) a year. If, then, you still haven't invested a full 15 percent of your income, add more to your pretax 401(k), 403(b), or other savings plan.

What if your employer doesn't match? First, fully fund the Roth IRA because of its flexibility. Then, put the rest of your 15 percent into your pretax 401(k), 403(b), SEPP, or 457. It may sound a little complicated, but let's see where you can end up.

Say J. G. and Jill make $40,000 a year when they turn thirty and they start saving $332 a month (that's $4,000 a year) in a Roth IRA. At 70½ years old, they will be required to begin withdrawing from their IRA. If they have invested in growth stock mutual funds with an average return of 12 percent per year, they will find $3,921,669, tax free, waiting for them. Wow!

But wait—our rule is to contribute 15 precent of our gross household income into retirement. Fifteen percent of $40,000 is $6,000 per year. That means J. G. and Jill have put another $2,000 into their 401(k) plan annually. Invested at a 12 percent annual return, that's another $2 million when they turn seventy. With our plan, they will retire with almost $6 million—almost $4 million of which is tax free. This is fun!

Of course, you will fund these plans by investing in mutual funds with five-plus-years proven track records and from the four categories we discussed in the investment chapter. If you follow this advice, you will change your family tree and live in a higher tax bracket in retirement than you are living now—another reason for the Roth. Go get 'em!

College Planning

Unfortunately, parents don't save for their children's college education any better than they do for their own retirement. According to the Gallup and Robinson poll quoted in *USA Today*, 80 percent of parents believe a college education is vital to their child's economic well-being. Yet only 48 percent have saved 1 to 50 percent of the cost. (Seven percent have saved 100 percent; and 22 percent have saved nothing.)

Wake-up Call!

The increase in college tuition outpaced inflation in the 1996–97 school year, according to a September 26, 1996, *New York Times* report. Public four-year college and university tuition increased 6 percent; private four-year tuition rose 5 percent.

As expensive as college can be these days, you can help send your kids to school by saving a little at a time, the same way you save for your retirement. In fact, the process of setting up a college fund is similar to that of creating a retirement plan. This time, however, we'll tackle the process in two steps: First, you dream; then, you create the monthly savings plan.

Step 1: Establish the Dream

Take time to dream about your kids' future and the kind of school you'd like them to be able to attend. If your children are thirteen or older, they can help you in this process. Talk with them about what they would like to do when they grow up so you can get an idea of the kind of education they might need.

Then, record their dreams and goals, and your dreams, in the spaces below.

What kind of career might your child want to pursue?

_____

_____

_____

_____

What kind of education would that require?

_____

_____

_____

_____

Do you plan to save for public or private college?

_____

_____

Call several state and private schools and ask for the tuition rate. Record the costs below:

School	Tuition

Barry and Emily were realistic in their expectations: Even though Luke was only ten, it was late to start saving for his college tuition. They might be able to do more for their girls—Ellie, aged eight, and Megan, aged six—because they were younger. But in the end, they agreed to create a college fund that would pay for a public school's tuition for each child. If the kids wanted to go to a school that cost more than the budget, they would have to pay the balance or seek out whatever scholarships were available.

Step 2: Create a Monthly Savings Plan

Now it's time to turn those dreams for your kids into reality by determining how much you need to save monthly for each child's tuition. As with the retirement savings plan, you have to determine the total nest egg; then, multiply by a factor that accounts for inflation to get your monthly savings.

1. *Determine the nest egg needed in today's dollars.* According to the *College Board Annual Survey of Colleges*, tuition has increased an average of 6 percent per year for public institutions and 5 percent per year for private institutions. So you'll need to figure in the cost of inflation when determining how much your child's tuition may be.

The table below reflects the average cost of tuition for a child entering an in-state college in the year 1996–97 and the projected costs for a child entering college eighteen years from now, in the year 2016.

	1996–97	2016
Public, four-year	$ 3,000	$ 8,000
Private, four-year	$13,000	$31,000
Public, two-year	$ 1,400	$ 4,000
Private, two-year	$ 7,000	$17,000

These figures, based on the average 1996–97 tuition fees posted in the *College Board Annual Survey of Colleges*, have been rounded off to the nearest thousand and do not include room and board.

Barry and Emily's children would enter college before the year 2016.

Nevertheless, they decided to save as if their children's tuition would be $8,000 per year. (Better to have more than less, they figured.) To determine the cost of four years of college, they simply multiplied by four:

$$\$8,000 \quad \times \quad 4 \qquad = \quad \$32,000$$
$$\text{Annual tuition} \quad \times \quad \text{\# of years} \quad = \quad \text{Nest egg needed}$$

Their $32,000 nest egg for each child would likely provide part of their room and board as well as their tuition.

2. *Calculate the monthly savings.* Choose the 8 percent factor (which accounts for the total earnings on a 12 percent mutual fund after inflation) for your child's age from the table on page 182. Then multiply your nest egg times the factor to get your monthly savings. Barry and Emily multiplied the $19,000 nest egg by the 8 percent factor for each of their children's ages.

$$\text{Luke, 10} \quad \$32,000 \times .007470 = \$239.04$$
$$\text{Ellie, 8} \quad \$32,000 \times .005466 = \$174.91$$
$$\text{Megan, 6} \quad \$32,000 \times .004158 = \$133.06$$

Compare the difference in the monthly amounts and you can see what a difference it makes when you put off saving for your child's tuition costs. Barry and Emily have to save almost twice as much for Luke, who is ten, as they do for Megan, who is only six.

Wake-up Call!

According to the College Board's annual report, *Trends in Student Aid: 1986–1996*, federal, state, and institutional sources made $50.3 billion available to students and their families in 1995 and 1996 to help with tuition, fees, and other expenses. Your child can find a way to go to college.

---

8 Percent Factors for College Savings

Child's Age	Years to Save	Factor
0	18	.002083
2	16	.002583
4	14	.003247
6	12	.004158
8	10	.005466
10	8	.007470
12	6	.010867
14	4	.017746

Now, using the factors in the table for college savings above, determine how much you will have to save for your child's college tuition.

1. Determine the nest egg.

$$\underline{\hspace{4cm}} \times \quad 4 \quad = \quad \underline{\hspace{4cm}}$$

      College tuition   Years   Nest egg needed

2. Calculate how much you need to save monthly.

Child 1

$\underline{\hspace{3cm}}$ $\times$ $\underline{\hspace{3cm}}$ $=$ $\underline{\hspace{3cm}}$

Nest egg $\times$ 8% factor by age $=$ Monthly savings

Child 2

$\underline{\hspace{3cm}}$ $\times$ $\underline{\hspace{3cm}}$ $=$ $\underline{\hspace{3cm}}$

Nest egg $\times$ 8% factor by age $=$ Monthly savings

Child 3

$\underline{\hspace{3cm}}$ $\times$ $\underline{\hspace{3cm}}$ $=$ $\underline{\hspace{3cm}}$

Nest egg $\times$ 8% factor by age $=$ Monthly savings

"All of these formulas are great for the planning process," you may be saying. "But how am I supposed to put the plan into action? How will I save for the kids to be educated as well as for retirement." That's what Barry and Emily wondered. After they completed their calculations, they realized they needed to save about $547 a month in the college fund. They had freed up $900 a month by completing their debt snowball, but they had just determined they needed to save almost $600 a month for their retirement. Their solution was to start saving $600 a month immediately for their retirement and putting $300 a month into their children's college fund. The good news for them was Barry eventually got a higher-paying job, which helped them save the other $247 a month.

Don't panic if you can't afford the amount you need to save. Remember, save for your retirement first. Then set aside what you can for your children's college education. Look for a higher-paying job; make the kids put part of their summer earnings into a mutual fund for their college tuition; help them look for scholarships. Together, you can make college a possibility.

How Does Your College Fund Grow? Baby Step 5

If—and only if—you are saving 15 percent of your income for your retirement, then it is time to take baby step 5.

Save for your kids' college education.

The 1997 tax-law-investment changes allow you to save up to $500 per child per year in an after-tax investment that grows tax free. These so-called education IRAs allow you to partially fund your child's college education with tax-free growth. If you save $500 per year ($41.67 per month) for eighteen years in a typical growth stock mutual fund at a 12 percent return per year, you will have approximately $32,000. By most estimates, that will cover the cost of four years at the average state school eighteen years from now (2016). This provision of the tax code is only for married couples who make less than

$150,000 annually and singles who make less than $95,000 annually in the year of the contribution. So when saving for college, you should first fully fund the $500 per child per year in a good growth mutual fund in the child's name. What about additional savings for living expenses or more expensive colleges? Glad you asked.

The best way to save more—and you should if you can—is by investing in a growth stock mutual fund using the Uniform Gift to Minors Act (UGMA) or the Uniform Transfer to Minors Act (UTMA). Your state law will dictate which of these apply. These provisions simply allow you to open a mutual fund in the child's name with you as the custodian (manager/decision maker) until the child reaches adulthood. These are after-tax investments that grow at the child's tax rate, which is nothing until the fund has some substantial money in it. Since you pay what little tax there is as it grows, there is no additional tax at withdrawal. There is no limit to what you can put into the child's name annually; however, if you put in more than $10,000 in one year you may be subject to gift tax. Avoid using zero coupon bonds or U.S. savings bonds for college saving. Although they grow tax deferred, the rate of return is half the typical mutual fund. Also, never invest for anything, even college, using a life insurance policy.

The tax act of 1997 will also allow you to take some tax credits as you pay college expenses. You get a tax credit (reduction in the actual taxes you pay) of $1,500 for the first $2,000 in expenses you pay per child annually for the first two years of college (freshman and sophomore). For all years after that, including graduate school and adult education, you receive a tax credit of 20 percent or a maximum of $1,000 of the first $5,000 spent annually. This credit is available only to couples making less than $80,000 annually and singles making less than $50,000 annually.

Keep in mind that, as the parent or grandparent, you are the manager, the custodian, of your child's money until he or she reaches eighteen. It's up to you to train your children to manage their money before they turn eighteen and receive their inheritance. If you don't, they will likely squander their money.

The Peace Track

Baby Step Checkup

Proverbs 13:22 says, "A good man leaves an inheritance for his children's children, but a sinner's wealth is stored up for the righteous." The first step in leaving future generations is to save for your retirement and your children's college education. Start moving forward on baby steps 4 and 5 this month. Remember, if you have to choose between saving for retirement and your children's college, save for retirement first.

Baby Step	Done	Action Needed to Complete	Date
1. Save $1,000 in an emergency fund.			
2. Pay off all debt using the debt snowball.			
3. Complete your emergency fund by saving three to six months' expenses.			
4. Invest 15 percent of your gross household income in Roth IRAs and pretax retirement plans.			
5. Save for your kids' college education.			

It's likely that by now you have used your cash-flow plan for one or two months. Take time this week to look over it and see how you will fit retirement and college saving into your plan, if you haven't already started saving for those categories. Talk with a friend or your spouse about how you may need to cut back on spending in order to save.

Weekly Goals

	Goal	Date
Spiritual		
Relational		
Physical		
Mental		

Protect Your Investments— and Your Loved Ones: Insurance

SAY THE WORD *insurance,* and watch people run for cover. It's a great way to clear a room at a party. Few other subjects engender the same feelings of confusion, frustration, and all-out distaste—not that it's hard to understand why. Stiff competition in the industry has given rise to more options and price ranges. The same policies can vary by hundreds of dollars, depending on the company. And if you don't know what you're looking for, you can buy more coverage than you need and miss out on significant discounts.

I wasn't surprised when Kit admitted the first time we talked about insurance that she hated even thinking about it. "I usually just close my eyes, point to a plan, and sign on the dotted line," she confessed. "That's how I chose our health insurance and our condo insurance. But for the past two years, since Monroe and I divorced, I have put off buying life insurance because I hate the process. The one salesperson I did talk to was pushy and threw at least ten plans at me to choose from. How was I supposed to know which was best?"

Although their insurance needs differed from Kit's, Barry and Emily, J. G. and Jill, and Dennis expressed similar frustrations. "There are so many kinds of insurance these days," J. G. said, "that I don't always know what's important anymore and I always feel ripped off when I finally do buy some."

As tempting as it can be to give in to the confusion and avoid buying insurance at all, insurance provides an important hedge against the risk of loss of income or property by transferring the risk to an outside source. So when those things that "will never happen to you" happen, someone else helps foot the bill and you don't wind up declaring bankruptcy.

Wake-up Call!

According to the Bankruptcy Institute, more than 50 percent of consumers go broke because of medical bills. What would have happened if those consumers had had adequate insurance in place to cover their bills?

Although there are entire books on the subject of insurance, we will examine the five basic kinds of insurance, what they protect, and how much you need:

1. Life insurance
2. Health insurance
3. Disability insurance
4. Homeowners or renters insurance
5. Automobile insurance

Life Insurance

Life insurance is really death insurance: It protects your family by replacing the cost of what you do—whether it's work in a corporate office or stay at home with the kids—if you die. Of course, we sugarcoat the name, calling it "life" insurance, because no one likes to think about death, especially their own. (That's a big reason people put off writing their wills.)

Single people with no dependents can afford not to think about life insurance; all they really need is a $20,000 policy that will cover their funeral expenses and any unpaid debts. On the other hand, for couples and parents of dependent children, it's poor planning, even irresponsible, not to protect your family in case you die.

Terms to Know

Cash-value insurance: Whole-life and universal, or variable, life insurance fall in this category. These policies sound attractive because they provide a savings program. But you can only buy them for life, they are costly, and the savings programs usually yield poor returns, around 3 percent for whole-life policies. Universal policies project better returns, around 9 or 10 percent, but they seldom reach that. In fact, the five-year track records of many universal-life policies don't even stack up against that of a CD. What you wind up with: an expensive insurance and a mediocre savings.

Term insurance: You can buy term policies for a specific period of time, say ten or twenty years, instead of for life; so you don't have to pay into them for life. They are also less expensive because there is no built-in savings program.

Guaranteed-renewable coverage: That means if you buy a twenty-year policy, the insurance company has to renew your policy for as long as you want. They can't keep you from purchasing another policy, even if you have acquired a terminal disease.

Level, or fixed-rate: This applies to term insurance in particular. When you buy a term policy, you lock in at a particular rate, which you pay until the policy expires. If you renew your policy, however, the rates will be higher, depending on your age.

Getting the Best Deal

Of the two types of insurance, term is the only one worth having. Why? Because it provides what you need when you need it: the most coverage while you and your family are young, for the best rate. A thirty-year-old will pay as much as 70 percent less for low-cost, fixed-rate (or level) term insurance than he or she will for whole- or universal-life policies. That gives you more money to invest while you are young. Term rates increase if you have to renew your policy when you get older. But if you save consistently in your emergency fund and in your 401(k), you won't need as much insurance when you are older. In fact, if you save enough, you can eventually become self-insured—that is, you won't need life insurance at all because your dependents will be able to support themselves on your savings.

Other drawbacks to cash-value policies:

- *Whole-life insurance pays only the "face" value when you die.* If you terminate the policy, you reap the cash value; but if you die, the company gets the savings, or cash value. For example, say you and your spouse buy a $70,000 whole-life policy and pay on it for ten years. At the end of the ten years, you may have an $8,000 cash value. If you die, the insurance company will pay your wife or husband $70,000, and they keep the $8,000.
- *Whole- or universal-life policies can cost more than you realize.* For one, you typically pay a fee to invest through a policy. According to *Worth* magazine, the commission you pay for a whole- or universal-life policy is typically 100 percent of the first year's premium—far more than you would ever pay a mutual fund if you invested yourself.

Kit had a whole-life policy while she and Monroe were married and wasn't interested in another one. "The agent who sold us the whole-life policy told us we would benefit from some savings plan it had," she said when she came to my office for help. "But when we canceled the policy during our divorce proceedings, we got a mere pittance of savings back. All those years of putting money into that policy with nothing to show for it—"

So she decided to go with a low-cost, level (fixed-rate) term insurance—the only way to go.

How Much Do You Need?

Using the worksheet on page 194 and the table of approximate term insurance costs on page 192, you can calculate how much insurance you need and the approximate annual premium.

Wake-up Call! 🐓

In his book *What Is a Wife Worth?*, author Michael Harry Minton applied national-average wages to the average amounts of time homemakers spend performing their daily tasks, such as household purchaser, maintenance worker, housekeeper, bookkeeper, nurse, dietitian, child psychologist, public relations/hostess. The total cost of services provided: $108,048.73 per year.

Important to keep in mind:

- *Cover your stay-at-home spouse.* Even if he or she doesn't earn an income, you will still need to replace what that person does, particularly if he or she is the primary caretaker of the children.
- *Get coverage for as long as the kids will be around.* A forty-year-old with almost-grown children, like Kit, will likely want only a ten-year policy. Even though they don't have children, a young couple, such as J. G. and Jill, will want a longer-term policy—say twenty or thirty years.
- *You need more than one year's salary.* Married couples and parents with dependent children need a policy worth about eight to ten times the salary of the spouse being covered. That way your spouse will be covered until he or she can find the necessary job or help. For example, if you make $40,000 a year and you buy a policy that is worth ten times your salary, $400,000 will go to your spouse if you die. The $400,000 invested at 10 percent will provide your spouse with $40,000 a year until the children grow up and beyond.
- *Single people with no dependents, like Dennis, and children need only enough coverage to pay their funeral expenses.*

Using this information, Kit filled out the life insurance worksheet on page 193. She determined that a ten-year policy would cover her long enough to provide for her daughters' education if something happened to her. ("If they go to graduate school, they'll have to pay for it," she declared.) She also decided she wanted eight times her income, or a $240,000 policy. To calculate her premium, she referred to the cost chart (below) and found that, for someone her age, insurance costs about $3.20 per $1,000 of coverage. Her math showed that her annual premium would be about $768 a year, or $64 a month.

Approximate Term Insurance Costs
Age 30—$1.70 per $1,000 in coverage
Age 40—$3.20 per $1,000 in coverage
Age 50—$8.00 per $1,000 in coverage
Age 60—$23.00 per $1,000 in coverage

By the time she turns fifty, Kit won't have to provide for her daughters anymore so she can buy a $20,000 policy, which will cover her funeral expenses. Her cost would be about $160 a year, or $13.33 a month. Then she can invest the extra $50 a month in a 12 percent mutual fund for retirement. Or, even better, if she has saved $20,000, she can drop all life insurance and invest the $768 a year she used to put toward life insurance.

You must be wary of life insurance agents. They aren't out to get you; they aren't bad people. But they do know that the commissions are higher on whole-life and universal-life insurance, which motivates them to push those products. You will have to stand your ground when you meet with the agents and insist that you have chosen term insurance.

Health Insurance

Most people who work in a company with twenty or more employees receive health insurance through their company. But whether you are insured by your employer or you have to go the more costly route of providing it for yourself, you need to be aware of your options and what the various plans provide.

Life Insurance Worksheet

Answer the following questions to help you determine how much insurance you need:

Are you married? Single? __Single__
Do you have dependent children? _Yes_ How many? __2__
How old are you? ____42____
How old are your children?

    ____16____

    ____19____

    _____

    _____

What is your gross income?
    Spouse 1: ___$30,000___
    Spouse 2: _____

Calculate the amount of insurance you want to buy for each spouse:
Spouse 1:

_$30,000_	×	__8__	=	_$240,000_
Income	×	(8–10)	=	Policy face value

Spouse 2:

$_____	×	_____	=	$_____
Income	×	(8–10)	=	Policy face value

Calculate your premiums:
Spouse 1:

_$240,000_	÷	_$1,000_	=	_$240_	×	_$3.20_	=	_$768_
Face value	÷	$1,000	=	Rate/$1,000	×	Cost	=	Premium

Spouse 2:

_____	÷	_$1,000_	=	_____	×	____	=	_____
Face value	÷	$1,000	=	Rate/$1,000	×	Cost	=	Premium

Life Insurance Worksheet

Are you married? Single? _____

Do you have dependent children? _____ How many? _____

How old are you? _____

How old are your children?

_____

_____

_____

_____

What is your gross income?

    Spouse 1: _____

    Spouse 2: _____

Calculate the amount of insurance you want to buy for each spouse:

Spouse 1:

_____	×	_____	=	_____
Income	×	(8–10)	=	Policy face value

Spouse 2:

$_____	×	_____	=	$_____
Income	×	(8–10)	=	Policy face value

Calculate your premiums:

Spouse 1:

_____	÷	$1,000	=	_____	×	_____	=	_____
Face value	÷	$1,000	=	Rate/$1,000	×	Cost	=	Premium

Spouse 2:

_____	÷	$1,000	=	_____	×	_____	=	_____
Face value	÷	$1,000	=	Rate/$1,000	×	Cost	=	Premium

Terms to Know

Health Maintenance Organizations (HMOs): Doctors who are prepaid by insurance companies for providing their health services. A form of "managed health care" (a four-letter word among some physicians), HMOs include groups of doctors who work in the same practice or individual physicians who join a network.

Preferred Provider Organizations (PPOs): My insurance broker says getting a PPO is like getting two health insurance plans in one: You get a minor medical insurance, which usually requires you to pay a small fee for minor health care services, such as annual checkups, and major medical insurance, which covers major health services, such as surgery and hospitalization, and requires you to pay between 10 and 30 percent of the fees for those services. Many people like PPOs because you can choose one of many doctors in a large network, provided by the PPO. The HMOs tend to be more restrictive about which doctors you see and when you see them.

Primary Care Physician (PCP): HMOs and PPOs typically require that you have a general practitioner as your PCP. He or she is responsible for evaluating you before you seek the care of a specialist and also for recommending the specialist you seek.

In-Network: Benefits that apply to employees who seek the care of a physician within the managed care network of doctors. Even PPOs have a network of doctors to choose from.

Out-of-Network: Benefits for those who seek medical providers outside the managed care network.

Coinsurance: Your out-of-pocket fee for the physicians' services after meeting your deductible.

Deductible: Your out-of-pocket cost before insurance is required to pay.

Stop-loss, or out-of-pocket: The most amount of money you have to pay out of pocket for your health insurance. If your stop-loss is $5,000 and you are on an 80-20 coinsurance plan, you have to pay 20 percent of your health care costs up to $5,000. After that, the insurance company pays 100 percent up to your lifetime maximum.

Getting the Best Deal

There are three ways you can save if you are insured by your employer:

1. *Go with the HMO.* You have more choice of physicians with the PPO, but you pay for your freedom.
2. *Read your policies carefully.* Double-income couples who are insured by their separate employers do not receive twice the care of singles. Rather, the insurers pay up to the most coverage allowed. For example, you may have an 80-20 co-pay plan and a physician's bill of $1,000. You have already met your deductible, so the insurance company will pay $800 of the bill. Your spouse has a 90-10 co-pay; so you can file a claim on your spouse's insurance, but it will only cover another 10 percent, or $100—not the rest of the bill. That means it's important that you carefully read both policies to determine whose policy provides the most coverage and go with that plan.
3. *Open a flexible spending account.* Some companies offer flexible spending accounts, which allow employees to save pretax dollars for their unreimbursed annual medical expenses, such as pregnancy checkups and routine checkups for babies and children. The trick is you have to estimate at the beginning of the year how much you will spend on your doctors' appointments, and you forfeit the money at the end of the year if you don't use it all. You can't roll the money over to the next year.

For the self-employed, selecting a health insurance plan gets tricky. Consider Dennis's experience. When he was first laid off, he was able to buy insurance through his company for eighteen months because of a federal law called COBRA (the Consolidated Omnibus Budget Reconciliation Act of 1985), which requires employers to offer group coverage to workers who have been laid off. The company no longer pays your premiums, or any part of them, but COBRA can be less expensive—though not always—than buying your own.

When Dennis's eighteen months were up, it was time to look for his own health insurance. He considered going without coverage—at least until his business was better established. He worked out regularly and never smoked; he didn't have any history of heart disease or cancer. Even so, he had no savings to cover medical expenses; if he needed to be hospitalized suddenly, the expense would ruin him financially.

If, like Dennis, you must provide your own health insurance, there are ways to save on your premiums:

- *Go with high deductibles.* By choosing a $1,000 instead of a $250 deductible, Dennis was able to save $100 a month.
- *Increase your co-pay.* Instead of paying 10 to 20 percent on your coinsurance, choose an 80-20 co-pay plan, or even a 70-30 if available. Depending on your age, an 80-20 could save as much as $200 a month on your premium.
- *Buy catastrophic coverage only.* Pay for dental and eye checkups out of pocket.

Using the savings on your health premiums, you can start a fund that's separate from your emergency fund to pay for deductibles.

One health insurance no-no: Never decrease the lifetime maximum pay from the insurance company below $1 million. You can't begin to anticipate what kinds of illnesses you or your family may battle in a lifetime. You don't want your coverage to run out.

How Much Do You Need?

There are no formulas to help you choose the health coverage you need. If you are insured by your employer, you will likely be able to choose between an HMO or a PPO with an in- or out-of-network physician. Employers often hand out comparison-of-benefits charts like the one that follows to help you decide which plan you want.

The amounts and percentages in the chart are similar to those in many plans, though the rates do vary from insurer to insurer. In this case, choosing a doctor outside the PPO network means the insurer pays 80 percent of your medical expenses after you reach the deductible; you pay 20 percent. The

Health Insurance Comparison of Benefits

Features	HMO	PPO	
		In-Network	**Out-of-Network**
Annual Deductible			
Individual	N/A	N/A	$200
Family	N/A	N/A	$500
Emergency Care			
Office	$10 per person	$10 per person	30% of charges
Hospital	$50 per person	$50 per person	$50 per person
Preventive Care	$10 co-pay	$10 co-pay	Ineligible
X ray & Lab	100%	90%	80%
Hospitalization	100% if arranged or authorized by PCP	90% if arranged or authorized by PCP	Subject to deductible, coinsurance, and precert
Surgical	100% if arranged or authorized by PCP	90% if arranged or authorized by PCP	Subject to deductible, coinsurance, and precert
Prescription drugs			
Generic	$5 co-pay	$5 co-pay	Separate $50 deductible, then 80% benefit
Brand Name	$10 co-pay	$10 co-pay	
Out-of-Pocket Maximum	N/A	$1,000 individual $2,000 family	$2,000 individual $5,000 family
Lifetime Maximum	Unlimited	Unlimited	$1 million

out-of-network plan also requires you to pay for 80 percent of the cost of drugs after you reach a $50 deductible. Some plans offer only 70 percent coverage, and you pay 30 percent. Also, some health insurance providers offer higher out-of-pocket maximums. No matter what company you choose, though, the one similarity is HMOs typically cost less for the insured than PPOs. Note that in the chart, the HMO provides 100 percent coverage for most medical expenses, except for the co-payments on doctor's-office and emergency-room visits and drugs.

If you must self-insure, then take time to comparison shop for your health coverage. Create a chart like the one on page 198, or fill in the Health Insurance Comparison of Benefits provided (page 200). Consider at least two or three plans; then record each plan's benefits in the chart. The categories of Outpatient and Inpatient Mental Health Care and Substance Abuse are included in the chart. Insurance companies differ in their coverage of these categories, so be sure to check each plan carefully to see what they offer. The Health Insurance Comparison of Benefits also includes a space for you to record the annual premiums and stop-losses. Fill in the name of the provider and the type of plan in the top row.

Just because a plan is less expensive doesn't mean you should choose that plan. Make sure you are comfortable with the physicians and the hospitals approved by the plan. You need to feel good about the care you receive as well as the cost of the insurance.

Disability Insurance

People often view disability insurance as an unnecessary expense. Don't make that mistake. Your chances of becoming disabled before you retire are far greater than your chances of dying before sixty-five. Yet, like most people, you probably own life insurance but no disability. Disability pays up to 55 percent of your current income if an injury or illness renders you unable to work. So it pays to purchase this overlooked insurance. (Believe me, you will rarely hear me encourage people to buy more insurance. But this is one occasion that warrants it.)

Health Insurance Comparison of Benefits

Features			
Annual Deductible *Individual* *Family*			
Emergency Care *Office* *Hospital*			
Preventive Care			
X ray & Lab			
Hospitalization			
Surgical			
Mental health care *Outpatient* *Inpatient*			
Substance Abuse			
Prescription drugs *Generic* *Brand Name*			
Out-of-Pocket *Maximum*			
Lifetime Maximum			
STOP-LOSS			
ANNUAL PREMIUM			

Terms to Know

Occupational disability: Offers specific coverage in case you can't perform the job you were educated or trained to do. For example, if you were trained to be a neurosurgeon and you cut a nerve in your hand so you couldn't perform surgery again, occupational disability would pay you according to your former income.

Elimination period: Similar to a deductible, the elimination period is the amount of time that lapses after your injury or disability and before the insurance company begins to pay you.

Getting the Best Deal

The cost of your premium is determined by the risk level the insurer assigns to your occupation and the elimination period you choose. Someone who works around large machinery will have higher premiums than, say, J. G., whose job as a loan officer poses a marginal health threat. You can save on your premiums, however, by lengthening your elimination period. The chart below illustrates how much J. G. and Kit can save by waiting longer before their disability benefits kick in.

Name	Occupation	Income	Monthly Coverage	Elimination Periods & Premiums*			
				30	60	90	180
J. G.	Loan officer	$40,000	$1,825	$93.99	$42.55	$38.82	$26.30
Kit	Admn. asst.	$30,000	$1,375	$150.00	$104.37	$72.47	$63.48

* Costs from a randomly selected insurance company.

Note that the 180-day elimination period costs almost half of what the thirty-day period costs. You can also see how the different risk levels of Kit's and J. G.'s jobs affect their premiums. J. G. gets more coverage for less than Kit because her job as administrative assistant carries a risk of carpal tunnel syndrome.

If you haven't completed your emergency fund, it may benefit you to pay the higher premiums for the thirty-day period at first. Then, when you have saved more, you can lengthen the period.

Keep in mind that your age, where you live, and your lifestyle (whether you smoke, for example) all play a part in the cost of your premiums.

How Much Do You Need?

How much disability insurance you purchase is based on your occupation and income. Use the chart provided to help you shop for disability insurance. Like the chart that shows the cost of J. G.'s and Kit's premiums, there is room for you to fill in your occupation, salary, the insurer's suggested coverage, and the premiums for the various elimination periods. There is space for you to record costs from three companies. Or you can use the space to fill in the costs for your spouse, if you are married.

Name	Occupation	Income	Monthly Coverage	Elimination Periods & Premiums			
				30	60	90	180

Many employees buy disability insurance through their employers' health insurance provider. Just make sure you buy a policy that covers you until you reach age sixty-five, or for life, not a short-term disability policy, which will pay out for three to five years.

Homeowners and Renters Insurance

Whether you rent or own a home, you need insurance that covers what it would cost to replace your home and/or the "stuff" inside in the event of a fire, theft, or other natural disaster. J. G. and Jill had rented a small house for three years without any insurance coverage, assuming that their landlord's insurance would cover their possessions if stolen or burned. That's a common mistake that can have tragic consequences. Take the example of a client of mine.

In most states the landlord does not have an insurable interest in his tenants' possessions, so he can't insure their property. Unfortunately, my client didn't know that and failed to purchase his own insurance. When he lost everything in a fire, he went to his landlord, looking for his insurance check, but it wasn't there to give him. The landlord could replace the house, but he couldn't replace the tenants' belongings. It was a very sad day for the tenant.

The basic renters policy covers your possessions and you, for fire and theft. It also covers possessions, such as a bicycle or computer, that are stolen when off the property. The basic homeowners policy covers

- the dwelling
- other structures (such as a free-standing garage or tool shed)
- contents
- loss of use
- liability

Terms to Know

Contents: Your possessions.

Floater: Additional insurance that covers your possessions if their value exceeds the limits of your replacement policy.

Liability: Covers you in case someone brings a lawsuit against you because he slips and falls or otherwise gets hurt while on your property. Many homeowner's policies include $100,000 of liability for no charge.

Loss of use: Reimburses you for expenses you incur because you have to move out of the home for a while. Includes rent, dining out, extra dry cleaning.

Replacement-value insurance: Pays what it would cost to replace your home and the contents. This is the *only* type of insurance you should buy. Agents who have an ounce of integrity will sell only this type of insurance.

Umbrella policy: Provides extra liability. If someone is hurt on your property, and the medical bills are $150,000 and your liability is $100,000, the umbrella policy will pay the other $50,000. If your personal belongings are worth more than $200,000, you should get an umbrella policy.

Getting the Best Deal

Most insurance companies offer deductions for security systems and smoke detectors, nonsmokers, new homes, and people who buy both auto and home insurance from the same company. Some companies even offer discounts to people whose homes are close to fire departments. If the agents you call don't mention discounts, ask about them.

Other ways to save, according to the Insurance Information Institute, a nonprofit communications organization in New York, sponsored by the property/casualty industry, include the following:

- *Take preventative steps.* When buying a home, consider the cost of insuring it. Construction materials and design can cut your premiums from 5 to 15 percent, depending on where you live. In the East, for example, brick is better because it resists wind damage; in the West, frame houses are preferred because they hold up during earthquakes.
- *Insure the house, not the land.* Your land isn't going to be stolen or damaged by wind or fire, so don't include the value of the land when determining how much coverage you need.
- *Ask about senior discounts.* Homeowners who are fifty-five and older can receive up to 10 percent discounts from some companies. The reason: Retired people spend more time at home, which secures their homes

against intruders and fires. They also tend to take better care of their homes.

- *Look for group coverage.* Employers and alumni and business associations often work out package deals with insurance companies, which include discounts on homeowners insurance for members.
- *Ask about discounts for staying with the same company.* Insurers frequently reduce policies for clients who have been with their company three to five years or longer.

Also, ask about higher deductibles. According to the Insurance Information Institute, increasing your deductible from $250 to $1,000 can save you as much as 24 percent on your premiums. Increasing the deductible to $2,500 can save up to 30 percent.

How Much Do You Need?

The day after we talked about insurance at FPU, J. G. and Jill got serious about shopping for a renter's policy. But first they did some prep work.

Before you contact any insurance agents, there are three steps you should take:

1. *Take an inventory of your possessions.* Renters and homeowners, walk through the house with a videocamera or regular camera, and take pictures of your possessions. Open the drawers, closets, and cabinets, and film your silver, jewelry, and clothing; take shots of the artwork on the walls. This is for your benefit as much as it is for the insurance company's; after all, you'll have to know what to replace if you ever lose it. When you have finished, store the videotape or photographs in a safe-deposit box, away from the house.

Keep in mind that most renter's policies have limits on how much they cover if items are stolen: $1,000 for jewelry, $3,000 to $10,000 for computers, and $2,500 to $10,000 for silverware or flatware, according to the Insurance Information Institute. For most renters, that provides sufficient coverage. However, check your policy's limits. If your valuables are worth more than the limit, you may want to complete the contents inventory sheet on page 209, and consider buying additional coverage, called a *floater*.

2. *Homeowner, have your house appraised for what it would cost to rebuild the house today.* That means find out what the local building costs per square foot are; then, multiply the cost by the square footage of your house and subtract the value of the lot. Even if your house is brand-new, you likely can't rebuild it for what you paid for it.

3. *Complete the worksheet on page 208.* The questions will help you become aware of discounts that may apply to you. And you can use the contents inventory to list items that may not be covered by your deductible. That will help you decide whether you need to buy additional insurance. Use J. G. and Jill's worksheet, on page 207, as an example.

J. G. and Jill took this worksheet with them when they met with insurance agents to help them determine how much insurance they needed. Because they had $10,000 in their emergency fund, they decided they could cover a $1,000 deductible. The result: they saved $72 a year on their premium. They saved another $14 a year because of their security system and their non-smoking status.

The one area J. G. and Jill decided to spend a little extra: They bought a floater to cover the few pricey possessions they had listed in their contents inventory. They had received a few expensive wedding presents from relatives, and Jill had inherited an antique chest from her grandmother, which the couple wanted insured. The policies they looked at would cover the silverware, but not the antique or the painting. Anytime your possessions are worth more than an individual policy covers—say, the policy covers $5,000 worth of jewelry, but you have a piece worth $15,000—it's a good idea to buy an additional floater policy.

Take time to complete the Homeowners/Renters Insurance form on page 208 before you shop for insurance.

As you consider your needs, keep in mind that if you have $10,000 in an emergency fund, you can get a larger deductible and save on your premiums. You can also start a separate fund to cover your insurance deductibles.

Homeowners/Renters Insurance

Do you rent? ___✓___ Own? _____
Are you a smoker/nonsmoker? _Nonsmokers_
How old are you? __25 and 27__
Have you completed your emergency fund? __yes__
Security:

    ___✓___ smoke detectors
    ___✓___ alarms
    ___✓___ dead bolts

Homeowners:

    Is your house urban/rural? _____
    How old is your home? _____
    Is the house brick or frame? _____
    Do you live in an area subject to

        _____ flooding
        _____ tornados/hurricanes
        _____ earthquakes

What kinds of sports or recreational equipment do you keep in the backyard?
(Example: pool, trampoline) _____

_____

_____

Appraisal notes:

_____ × _____ = _____ − _____ = _____
Sq. ft. × cost per sq. ft. = Cost to rebuild − Lot value   Coverage

_____ × _____ = _____ − _____ = _____
Sq. ft. × cost per sq. ft. = Cost to rebuild − Lot value   Coverage

Homeowners/Renters Insurance

Do you rent? _____ Own? _____
Are you a smoker/nonsmoker? _____
How old are you? _____
Have you completed your emergency fund? _____
Security:

       _____ smoke detectors

       _____ alarms

       _____ dead bolts

Homeowners:

     Is your house urban/rural? _____

     How old is your home? _____

     Is the house brick or frame? _____

     Do you live in an area subject to

         _____ flooding

         _____ tornadoes/hurricanes

         _____ earthquakes

What kinds of sports or recreational equipment do you keep in the backyard?
(Example: pool, trampoline) _____

_____

_____

Appraisal notes:

$$\underline{\hspace{2cm}} \times \underline{\hspace{3cm}} = \underline{\hspace{3cm}} - \underline{\hspace{2cm}} = \underline{\hspace{2cm}}$$

Sq. ft.   ×   cost per sq. ft.   =   Cost to rebuild   −   Lot value   Coverage

$$\underline{\hspace{2cm}} \times \underline{\hspace{3cm}} = \underline{\hspace{3cm}} - \underline{\hspace{2cm}} = \underline{\hspace{2cm}}$$

Sq. ft.   ×   cost per sq. ft.   =   Cost to rebuild   −   Lot value   Coverage

Contents Inventory

Item Description	Value
Silverware (12 5-pc. place settings), wedding present	$2,000
Oil painting, wedding present	$3,500
Antique china cabinet, 1850	$5,000
Stereo	$2,500

Contents Inventory

Item Description	Value

Auto Insurance

When it comes to buying auto insurance, you have a distinct disadvantage because most states require you to have it. That means you are at the mercy of the insurers. They can sell you coverage you don't really need and increase their rates at will. In fact, the average cost to insure an automobile rose 44 percent between 1987 and 1994 according to the January 1997 *Consumer Reports* magazine. Don't be discouraged, though. There are ways to save.

To start, your auto policy should cover the items under "Terms to Know."

Terms to Know

Bodily injury liability: Pays for injuries you cause to another person.

Collision: Covers the cost of repairing or replacing your car, regardless of whose fault the wreck is.

Comprehensive: Pays for damage to your car that doesn't involve a collision, such as theft, vandalism, fire, falling objects, hail, flood, earthquake.

Uninsured motorists coverage: Covers your car in the case of a collision with an uninsured motorist.

Property damage liability: Covers damage you cause to other cars or property while driving.

Getting the Best Deal

As with homeowners insurance, many companies offer discounts on auto insurance—especially if you have your homeowners and auto insurance with the same company.

Barry and Emily received a 15 percent reduction on their premium for three years of accident-free driving, and another 12 percent multicar discount because they had two cars on the same policy. They also received a 5 percent reduction because they had their home and auto insurance with the same insurer.

According to the Insurance Information Institute, insurance companies also frequently offer discounts for the following:

- *Antilock brakes (ABS):* Antilock brakes improve steering and control when a car comes to a sudden stop, reducing the number of wrecks. Some states, including Florida, New Jersey, and New York, require insurers to give antilock brake discounts. Other insurance companies offer an ABS discount nationwide.

- *Low mileage.*
- *"Low profile" cars:* Some cars are more vulnerable to theft than others; some are more expensive to repair. To see how various models of cars rate, you can write to the Insurance Institute for Highway Safety, 1005 North Glebe Road, Arlington, Virginia 33301, and ask for the Highway Loss Data Chart.
- *Automatic seat belts and air bags.*
- *Where you live:* Companies often charge less to insure cars in rural communities than those in urban areas where more break-ins occur and there is more traffic.
- *Security systems.*
- *Senior citizens.*
- *Good grades for students.*
- *Driver training courses.*

Some types of auto coverage you don't need, according to the January 1997 *Consumer Reports* magazine:

- *Medical, or in some states, personal injury protection (PIP):* Unless your state requires PIP, these are two payments you don't need. Your health insurance should adequately cover you and members of your household.
- *Glass breakage.*
- *Rental reimbursement and towing:* Only buy this type of coverage if you don't belong to an auto club, such as AAA, or don't have an emergency fund.

Wake-up Call!

Many people trade cars without considering what it will cost to insure the new car. Then they wind up in financial trouble, unable to make their payments. They say things like, "Dave, I could 'afford' the new payments; it was the insurance costs that got me." Always find out the cost of insurance on a new automobile before you buy.

How Much Do You Need?

A good rule of thumb when buying auto insurance is to buy high liability and high deductibles. Your policy should include bodily injury liability, collision, comprehensive, uninsured motorists coverage, and property damage. If it covers additional categories, you may be double-insuring yourself, so check your other insurance policies and get rid of what you already have covered.

Barry and Emily spent $1,200 a year in premiums on their two cars, so they were anxious to assess where they could cut back. Here's what their six-month coverages and limits included:

Liability:	
Bodily injury 100,000/300,000	
Property damage 25,000	$117.39
Medical payments 25,000	11.97
50 deductible comprehensive	40.74
250 deductible collision	102.69
Emergency road service	1.70
Car rental/travel expense	10.00
Uninsured motor vehicle:	
Bodily injury 100,000/300,000	
Property damage 25,000	24.60
Death indemnity	2.40

Surprisingly, the first thing Barry and Emily did was increase their coverage instead of decrease it. Like disability, liability insurance is a good buy—one of the best buys in insurance, in fact. Barry and Emily's 100,000/300,000 bodily injury liability coverage meant that their insurer would pay up to $100,000 of medical coverage per individual per accident and no more than $300,000 per accident. So if Barry had a wreck and three people were hurt, incurring medical bills of $500,000, the policy would cover only $300,000 and Barry would have to pay $200,000 out of pocket. If you know anything about the cost of hospitalization and medical bills, you know how expensive it can be. What's more, you have lawsuits to worry about. The hospitalization may only cost $300,000, but if you are at fault in a wreck that causes someone to become permanently disabled, he will surely sue you when he gets out of the hospital. In that kind of scenario, your 100,000/300,000 won't provide nearly enough coverage.

Similar to the bodily injury liability, the 100,000/300,000 uninsured motor vehicle bodily injury covers *your* medical expenses if an uninsured motorist hits you. Many insurers keep the bodily injury liability and the uninsured motor vehicle bodily injury the same—if you want to raise one, you have to raise the other. As a result of our conversation about insurance, Barry and Emily changed their two bodily injury coverages to $250,000 per person and $500,000 per accident. Their cost was only an additional $53 a year—not much compared to the hundreds of thousands of dollars you could someday have to pay out of pocket to cover someone else's or your own hospital bills.

Another way to address the issue of liability coverage is by purchasing an umbrella policy, which can cover you from $1 million and up in the event that you are held responsible for another person's physical injury. Depending on your age and where you live, umbrella policies can cost $111 and up. Again, that's a good deal compared to a million-dollar lawsuit.

Although Barry and Emily added $53 a year for the increased liability and uninsured motor vehicle bodily injury coverage, they were able to save by raising one of their deductibles. The 50 deductible comprehensive amount in Barry and Emily's policy indicates they are responsible for the first $50 of noncollision damage done to their car in a year; the insurer covers the rest.

Auto Insurance Worksheet

Name _____ Age _____

Female/Male _____ Married/Single _____

Are you a member of an auto club? _____

Who is your homeowners insurance provider? _____

Car Model	Year	# of Miles	Annual Mileage	Antilock Brakes	Automatic Seat Belts	Air Bags
Barry's car	1987	150,000	15,000		✓	
Emily's car	1995	20,000	10,000	✓	✓	✓

Do you have student drivers?

    Male/female _____ Age _____ GPA* _____

    Male/female _____ Age _____ GPA _____

    Male/female _____ Age _____ GPA _____

Have they had driver's training? _____

* GPA=grade point average

The 250 deductible collision indicates that Barry and Emily will have to pay $250 of collision damages in a year before the insurer pays for any collision damages. By raising their collision deductible to $1,000 on Emily's car—which reduced her premium by almost half—and dropping it altogether on Barry's car, an older model worth about $1,500, the couple was able to save almost $300 a year on their premiums. (You're not feeling so bad about raising your liability anymore, are you?) Collision insurance on older cars tends to be more than it's worth because you risk having your premiums increased every time you file a claim. If you have a $250 deductible and file a claim to repair a $500 dent, you will get a check for $250. But your premium may go up $200 a year as a result. So what have you gained, especially if, like Barry, you have an old car whose total value is low?

Barry and Emily cut back in some other categories also. When they examined their other insurance policies, they discovered that several categories on their policy were covered elsewhere, including medical payments, rental and towing, and death indemnity. As members of an auto club, they had free towing and emergency roadside service and inexpensive rental; so they didn't need rental or towing insurance. And death indemnity was a waste because it simply contributes toward funeral expenses, which their life insurance covered. So they discontinued the categories and invested the savings. (You may recall that in chapter 10 Barry and Emily needed $300 a month to save for their children's college education. They just made that amount by saving on their insurance!)

While they were shopping for auto insurance, Barry and Emily completed the auto insurance worksheet on page 214, which they took with them when they met with the agents. That way they had on paper the basic information to show what discounts they might qualify for (antilock brakes, air bags, low miles).

Before you change your insurance, complete the blank auto insurance worksheet provided on page 216. You can also use the following suggested *minimums* from the January 1997 *Consumer Reports* magazine to help you plan how much coverage you need:

- *Collision:* $500.
- *Comprehensive:* $500.
- *Uninsured motorists coverage:* $100,000 per person, $300,000 per accident.
- *Property damage liability:* Check your policy to see how much coverage you have. Most states require you to have at least $15,000 per accident, but you can buy up to $100,000.

Like Barry and Emily, you can take this worksheet with you when you meet with auto insurance agents. Be sure to check your other insurance policies so that you don't get double coverage on your car. You will be amazed at how much you can save when you thoroughly research and examine your policies.

Auto Insurance Worksheet

Name _____ Age _____

Female/Male _____ Married/Single _____

Are you a member of an auto club? _____

Who is your homeowners insurance provider? _____

Car Model	Year	# of Miles	Annual Mileage	Antilock Brakes	Automatic Seat Belts	Air Bags

Do you have student drivers?

Male/female _____ Age _____ GPA* ____

Male/female _____ Age _____ GPA ____

Male/female _____ Age _____ GPA ____

Have they had driver's training? _____   ° GPA=grade point average

---

Whom Do You Trust?

After you calculate how much insurance you need, you still have the important task of finding the right insurance company and the right policy. Many of the charts in this chapter are set up so you can do some comparative shopping.

In other cases, you will simply have to take good notes on another sheet of paper.

How do you find an insurance agent you can trust?

- *Seek referrals from friends and relatives.* J. G. asked his boss and his father for their agents' names and what kind of service they provided, such as how quickly they responded to claims. Jill called the Independent Insurance Agents Association for her state and asked for the names of three reputable agents in her area. She also could have called the state insurance department for a referral, though she chose not to because of time constraints. The numbers for each state's insurance department are in the appendix on pages 256 and 257.
- *Look for an agent with whom you can develop a comfortable teacher-student relationship.* Your agent should educate you about the industry, what your options are, and what discounts are available.

By now, your head is probably spinning. The work may feel tedious, but the exercises and the information will help you later as you shop for the best deals. Remember, insurance protects you against the risk of catastrophic loss. Despite what the insurance agents out there may tell you, you *can* have too much insurance. And you pay too much for it for you to be an insurance ostrich—that is, someone whose head is in the sand. The following types of insurance, in particular, are unnecessary and should be avoided at all costs:

- Cancer and hospital indemnity insurance
- Home office equipment insurance
- Credit card insurance
- Credit-life insurance
- Accidental death insurance
- Prepaid burial policies

In particular, credit life—life insurance offered by a lender to make sure your bills will be paid in the event of your death—is one of the most expensive, horrible kinds of life insurance there is. A lender cannot force you to buy this, so don't.

Don't be overwhelmed by the sheer complexity of unusual types of insurance. Remember the KISS principle I use for investing: Keep it simple, stupid! Keep your insurance premiums low and continue to save in your emergency fund. You will be ready for life's unexpected events.

The Peace Track

Baby Step Checkup

Proverbs 27:12 says, "A prudent man sees evil and hides himself; the naïve proceed and pay the penalty." You can hope for the best, but it's always wise

Baby Step	Done	Action Needed to Complete	Date
1. Save $1,000 in an emergency fund.			
2. Pay off all debt using the debt snowball.			
3. Complete your emergency fund by saving three to six months' expenses.			
4. Invest 15 percent of your gross household income in Roth IRAs and pretax retirement plans.			
5. Save for your kids' college education.			

to prepare for the worst. As you note where you are in the Baby Step Checkup, take time also to think about what kind of insurance coverage you may still need. Do you have life insurance that will take care of your family in case you die? What about health insurance?

Make it a goal this week to review your insurance policies with your spouse. If you have questions, call your agent and make sure you understand what you have.

Weekly Goals

	Goal	Date
Spiritual		
Relational		
Physical		
Mental		

TWELVE

To Buy or What to Buy?
Real Estate and Mortgages

"I CAN'T WAIT to get out of this house," Jill told J. G. "I'm so tired of renting a place where your neighbors can practically see in your back door—not to mention hear every move you make in the house."

"It has been frustrating," J. G. agreed. "What gets to me is the pressure our parents are putting on us to move. How many times do you think they've asked us, 'When are you going to buy? You're throwing your money down a rat hole by renting.' "

Like most Americans, J. G. and Jill dreamed of someday owning their own home. According to a 1994 Federal National Mortgage Association (FNMA, or Fannie Mae) poll, conducted by Peter Hart and Robert Teeter, 85 percent of eighteen- to twenty-four-year-olds and 56 percent of the sixty-five-plus group prefer to buy rather than to rent—and with good reason.

Aside from the appeal of having your own backyard where the 2.5 kids can play with their shaggy dog while you and your spouse grill burgers and have "quality time," residential real estate is a great investment. In fact, the appreciating value of a house makes buying one a key to building long-term wealth. Except for parts of California and the Rust Belt, most of the country has watched residential real estate double and triple in value over the past twenty-five years. As a result, houses have created a hedge against inflation.

In addition to being a great investment, your personal residence became an even more important investment with the advent of the 1997 tax-law changes. Now couples can sell their personal home every two years and make a tax-free profit of up to $500,000 (singles up to $250,000). Wow! This is yet another reason to have home ownership in your long-term plans. What's more, it allows some of you who want or need to move to a less expensive house and become debt free to do so without a tax penalty. Say, for example, you owe $80,000 on a $200,000 home. The kids have grown up and moved out, so you want to downsize. You can now buy a $120,000 home with your equity and pay zero tax. A debt-free home—I like it!

Just because a house is a great investment, though, doesn't mean it's time to buy—nor does it mean you should buy the "dream" house you want to retire in. Two of the most common first-time buyer mistakes are

- Buying too soon
- Buying more than you can afford, and so becoming house poor

There are steps you can take to prevent these errors. You can start by asking yourself some questions to determine whether the timing is right to buy a house.

When *Not* to Buy a House

As much as J. G. and Jill wanted a house, they also wanted to be sure they weren't buying a house too soon. They had just recovered from $26,000 of debt, so they didn't take debt lightly, even a mortgage. Dennis, on the other hand, was certain he was ready for home ownership.

Dennis wanted to buy a house now so he could someday move out and turn it into rental property. His long-term goal was to have a real estate portfolio of at least ten rental houses. The financing might be a problem, he thought, because he was starting a new business. But he was almost debt-free, and he figured he could find some creative financing that wouldn't require any down payment.

The following six questions will help you decide whether you are ready for home ownership.

1. *Are you going to move in the next five years?* Real estate is a good investment *if you hold on to it for at least five years.* Any less than that and the house in most areas won't appreciate enough to get your expenses out of it—i.e., you won't have any new equity in the house. That means it's not a good idea to buy when you are moving to a city on a temporary assignment or if there is a chance you could get transferred in the next one or two years.

2. *Is your life in a state of flux?* It's not a good idea to buy a house when you are right out of college, between jobs, or likely to marry but not yet engaged. That dream job you just interviewed for may fall through, and you may have to take a job in a different city. Or, as unbelievable as it seems, you could meet someone and get married in a year or two. If you have a house, your new bride or groom will inevitably hate it because he/she has different tastes from yours—that's Murphy's Law of real estate buying. Then, you'll be stuck in a house you both hate.

3. *Have you been married less than a year?* Married couples should wait at least a year before buying a house. That gives you time to figure out the perfect distance from the in-laws, as well as time to get to know each other, start defining your mutual tastes, pay off past debts, and save money. Don't get trapped by the "You're throwing your money down a rat hole" mentality. Patience pays.

4. *How much of a down payment do you have?* You need to have saved *at least* a 10 percent down payment before you start house hunting. Twenty percent is even better. That way you can avoid paying private mortgage insurance (PMI), which protects the mortgage company in case they have to foreclose on you and sell the house at a loss. PMI costs about $47 a month per $100,000 of loan, so you can save almost $600 a year on a $100,000 loan if you pay 20 percent down.

5. *Will you have to dip into the emergency fund for the down payment and closing costs?* Countless numbers of couples wind up in financial trouble because they use their emergency fund for the down payment. Or they'll use their VA benefit to put nothing down on a house, then spend their emergency fund on 90-days-same-as-cash furniture to dec-

orate the house. When you do that, you invite Murphy to move into your spare bedroom. Inevitably, someone gets laid off; and suddenly, you find yourself turning to the credit card or borrowing from the bank to meet your basic expenses. You may even have to sell your dream house, a sure way to lose money if you haven't had it long.

6. *Have you paid all your debts?* There's nothing like a case of house fever to get you motivated to pay your debt snowball! Don't even think about buying a house until you are completely out of debt.

After answering the above questions, J. G. and Jill pronounced themselves ready for home ownership. They planned on being in the same city for a while, possibly for a lifetime. They lived within two to three hours of each set of in-laws, so they felt comfortable about how close they were to their relatives. Plus, they had saved almost $12,000 for a down payment.

For Dennis, however, the list was a reality check. He was still convinced he could come up with creative financing so he wouldn't have to touch his emergency fund for a down payment. But when he studied his cash flow, he realized he was putting almost all of his cash into his business to get it off the ground. Trying to come up with the cash for a house *and* a new business would create a lot of pressure. As a result, Dennis wisely decided that until he could generate a steady income from his business, he would put off buying a house.

As you consider whether now is the time to buy a house, fill out the following checklist. Which statements are true of you?

___ You may move in the next five years.
___ Your life is in a state of flux.
___ You have been married less than a year.
___ You have not saved at least a 10 percent down payment on the house.
___ You have to dip into the emergency fund for the down payment and closing costs.
___ You still have debt.

Don't even think about venturing into home ownership if you checked any of the above statements. Instead, take time to set some goals that will help get you ready to buy. (Example: *Save $20,000 for a down payment by cutting back on entertainment and working extra.*) Create a realistic time line in which you can accomplish those goals.

Goal	Date to Accomplish
_____	_____
_____	_____
_____	_____
_____	_____

How Much Can I Afford?

During the first three years of their marriage, J. G. and Jill frequently spent Sunday afternoons driving through neighborhoods where they thought they would like to buy. They even met a real estate agent, who "prequalified" them for a loan—that is, she determined what she thought they could afford by pulling their credit reports and comparing their debts and income.

As agents and mortgage bankers typically do, J. G. and Jill's real estate agent estimated that they could pay $1,423.33—28 percent of their gross pay—a month in mortgage payments.

Wake-up Call!

If you want to achieve financial peace and build wealth, then you will never buy a house with a mortgage that's more than 25 percent of your take-home pay.

The 3 percent difference between the Financial Peace recommendation and what mortgage bankers and real estate agents will qualify you for is significant particularly because the Financial Peace recommendation is based on your *take-home pay*, not the *gross pay*. When they used the Financial Peace formula to determine how much of a monthly mortgage fee they could afford, J. G. and Jill figured out that they should be looking for houses with $1,042-a-month mortgage costs. (Twenty-five percent of their $50,000 annual take-home pay is $12,500, about $1,042 a month.)

J. G. and Jill were obviously disappointed when they realized they had to adjust their expectations and start looking for less house than they had hoped to buy. That's why it's helpful to figure out what you can afford *before you talk to a mortgage banker or real estate agent.* In fact, it's smart to figure out what monthly mortgage you can afford before you ever look at a house.

Determine how much mortgage you can afford to pay each month in the space below. All you have to do is multiply your monthly take-home pay by 25 percent. Refer to your budget on page 78 for your take-home-pay amount.

$$\underline{\hspace{3cm}} \quad \times \quad .25 \quad = \quad \underline{\hspace{3cm}}$$

Monthly take-home $\quad \times \quad .25 \quad = \quad$ Monthly mortgage

You may not like it in the short run, but in the long run, you will be better off living by the Financial Peace rule of real estate: Less is best—less mortgage, less time paying off the loan (fifteen years or less, to be exact), and lower interest rates.

Less Is More

Consider the savings if you were to finance an $80,000 home at 10 percent interest for fifteen years instead of thirty:

	# Payments	×	Monthly Mortgage	=	Total
30 years	360	×	$720	=	$252,720
15 years	180	×	$860	=	$154,800
YOU SAVE					$ 97,920

For $140 more a month, you can save almost $100,000. (You can scrape up $140 a month—you probably spend that much on pizza and bowling.) The result: After paying off your mortgage, you will have $860 a month you can invest in mutual funds for retirement or that honeymoon you never took because you were too broke when you first married. You may even be able to move up in house after you save awhile, this time paying cash.

Another strategy to keep in mind: Buy less house. Compare the difference in debt and equity after ten years when you purchase a $65,830 home on a thirty-year, 8.5-percent-interest loan to that of a $50,775 home on a fifteen-year, 8.5-percent-interest loan:

Mortgage	–	**Owe**	=	**Equity**
$65,830	–	$58,327	=	$ 7,503
$50,775	–	$24,370	=	$26,405

The monthly mortgage on the more expensive house is $600 a month, and the monthly mortgage on the less expensive house is $500. So if you invest the extra $100 a month in a 10 percent mutual fund, you would have a little more than $20,000. Your gain over the other house would be more than $46,000.

Back Into the Loan Amount

When J. G. and Jill realized the houses they had been looking at were out of their price range, they had to scale way back on their expectations for their first home. It was disappointing. There's nothing harder than looking at $100,000 houses and then finding out you can afford only an $80,000 house. But they had learned their lesson. They didn't want to make the same mistake twice, so they decided to determine exactly how much of a loan they could afford, using the loan factors chart on page 228.

The going interest rate on loans was 7.5 percent. So they divided the monthly payment they could afford, $1,041.67, by the 7.5 percent factor from the chart. That gave them the cost of the house per thousands. Then they multiplied that amount by 1,000 to get the cost of the house or the loan they could afford at the current interest rate. Their math looked like this:

$$\$1,041.67 \div 9.28 = 112.25 \times 1,000 = \$112,250$$

Mortgage payment ÷ Loan factor = Cost/1000s × 1,000 = Loan/House

With their $12,000 down payment, J. G. and Jill could afford a $124,000 house or less.

If you know the cost of the house or the amount of loan you would have to take out and you want to find out how much mortgage it would require, then simply work the problem backward. Divide the cost of the house or loan amount by 1,000 to get the cost per thousands. Then multiply by the fifteen-year factor for the current loan interest rate. For a $110,000 loan at 7.5 percent interest over fifteen years the math looks like this:

$$\underline{\$110,000} \div \underline{1,000} = \underline{110} \times \underline{9.28} = \underline{\$1,020.80}$$

Loan amt. ÷ 1,000 = Cost/1000s × Factor = Mortgage payment

You should use the loan factors chart on page 228 to figure out how much you can afford for a house. If you need to determine what a particular house's monthly payment would be, use the following formula:

$$\underline{\hspace{3cm}} \div 1,000 = \underline{\hspace{3cm}} \times \underline{\hspace{3cm}} = \underline{\hspace{3cm}}$$

Sales price ÷ 1,000 = Price @ 1,000 × Loan factor = Monthly payment

15- and 30-Year Loan Factors

Rate	15-Year	30-Year
4.5%	7.65	5.07
5%	7.91	5.37
5.5%	8.17	5.68
6%	8.44	6.00
6.5%	8.71	6.32
7%	8.99	6.66
7.5%	9.28	7.00
8%	9.56	7.34
8.5%	9.85	7.69
9%	10.15	8.05
9.5%	10.44	8.41
10%	10.75	8.78
10.5%	11.05	9.15
11%	11.37	9.52
11.5%	11.68	9.90
12%	12.00	10.29

On the other hand, if you need to figure out the total cost of the loan you can afford, use this equation:

$$\underline{\hspace{3cm}} \div \underline{\hspace{1cm}} = \underline{\hspace{2cm}} \times \underline{\hspace{1cm}} = \underline{\hspace{2cm}}$$

Mortgage payment ÷ Factor = Cost/1000s × 1,000 = Loan/House

Remember, you don't have to buy as much house as you can afford. Don't be ashamed to buy a little less and save the difference. Then you can buy a bigger house for cash.

Creative Financing

Getting the right financing is as important as deciding how much house you can afford. Here are four options to consider:

1. *Conventional loan.* You usually obtain conventional loans through the Federal National Mortgage Association (FNMA), which insures them against default. Down payments range from 5 to 20 percent or more, though the Financial Peace recommendation is a minimum of 10 percent.
2. *VA, or Veterans Administration loan.* The Veterans Administration insures these loans, which were designed to benefit veterans and allow a true zero-down purchase. Competitive interest rates make these appealing. But if you use them, remember to keep your loan to a fifteen-year minimum so you can pay off the house as quickly as possible.
3. *Owner financing.* If you are looking for creative financing, this is the way to go. Instead of paying a mortgage company, you pay the owner, who finances the purchase of his home. One benefit of owner financing is it provides flexibility in the way you pay off the loan. For example, if the house needs a lot of work, you may agree with the owner to forgo payments for a year so you can put your money into fixing up the house. Or you may decide to pay graduated interest rates or receive a discount for early payoff.
4. *Assumable loans.* These are pre-1986, fixed-rate FHA and VA loans, which can be assumed without any bank qualification. The buyer pays the seller the equity he has in the house and takes over the loan.

As long as the rates are competitive and the terms are for fifteen years or less, any of the above types of loans are acceptable ways of financing a mortgage. There are, however, two types of loans you should avoid: the *FHA, or Federal Housing Administration loan,* and the *ARM, or adjustable rate mortgage.*

The FHA loans, which are insured by the Department of Housing and

Urban Development (HUD), are appealing because they make it possible for people to put as little as 3 percent down on a house. However, what makes them appealing also makes them more expensive than conventional loans and, thus, not good deals.

Adjustable rate mortgages were the creation of struggling S and Ls in the late 1970s, during the Carter administration, when interest rates skyrocketed. While interest rates for CDs and money markets rose as high as 14 percent, the S and Ls still had 7 percent, fixed-rate real estate loans on their books. That meant they were paying out more to their customers than they were making. The S and Ls' solution was to devise the adjustable rate mortgage, which is based on indexes that rise and fall with the interest rates. Some of the most commonly used indexes for determining ARMs are the one-year Treasury bill (T-bill), the LIBOR (London Inter-Bank Offered Rate), and the Eleventh District Cost of Funds. Although they are sold as a way for buyers to get into a home because they often offer low initial rates, ARMs hold no benefit for the buyer, and, in fact, transfer all of the risk of borrowing to the buyer.

Adjustable Rate Rip-off

The first year Kit was divorced, she rented a condominium with both of her daughters. Even though her oldest, Malinda, went to college the second year, Kit still wanted to buy a small house for Terri and herself. Condo life made her feel closed in, and she didn't like some of the people Terri wound up hanging around with at the pool during the summer.

The divorce made it hard for Kit to get a loan, so she jumped when a mortgage banker offered her an ARM at a reduced rate of 5.75 percent for the first year. What she didn't count on was the rate going up the next year. As loan institutions frequently do, Kit's mortgage banker started her below the current adjustable rate, just to get her in the door. The only way the interest rate could stay the same the second year would be for the index to drop. Unfortunately for Kit, the index rose and so did her interest rate, from 5.75 percent to 7.75 percent.

Although it wasn't true of Kit, ARMs frequently appeal to immature buyers—people who want more than they can afford. If the only way you can afford the house of your dreams is by getting an adjustable rate mortgage, you know for sure you're buying way too much house.

Wake-up Call!

According to the FDIC, more than 35 percent of ARMs are adjusted incorrectly. So if you have one, check it to be sure it's correctly adjusted. If you want an audit of several years, then call the American Homeowners Association in Washington, D.C., 1-800-283-4887.

How to Adjust Your Own Mortgage

According to the *Wall Street Journal*, many financial institutions "forget" to lower an ARM when an index drops, though they rarely, if ever, "forget" to raise it. You can protect yourself, however, if you know how to figure the changes in your rates yourself. It's a simple three-step process:

1. Look at your note and find out what index you use and the date it is to be adjusted (usually the one-year anniversary of the closing date).
2. Find the margin assigned to your loan.
3. On the anniversary of your closing, look up the index in the *Wall Street Journal*. Add that index to your margin and you will have the new rate (if the margin is not capped).

Kit's index was the one-year, 4 percent T-bill; her margin, 2.59. The second year the one-year T-bill rose to 5.3 percent. That should have raised her interest rate to 7.89 percent. As with most ARMs, however, Kit's had a

2 percent annual cap. Since she started at 5.75 percent, her interest rate only went up to 7.75.

Take time to adjust your own mortgage rate, using the formula below.

$$\underline{\hspace{3cm}} \quad + \quad \underline{\hspace{3cm}} \quad \quad \underline{\hspace{3cm}}$$

$$\text{Index} \quad + \quad \text{Margin} \quad = \quad \text{Interest rate}$$

"If I had it to do over again," Kit confessed, "I would never let someone talk me into something so ridiculous. I can't believe how blind I was to the risks involved."

Lucky for Kit, she wasn't stuck. If you have an ARM, you can, and should, refinance the loan.

To Refinance or Not to Refinance

For anyone who has an ARM, refinancing is a must. You can do this either through a full refinance or through a conversion feature included in many ARM contracts. The latter option allows you to convert the loan to 0.25 to 0.5 percent above the market rate. Some ARMs even include a free conversion option, which means you pay between $250 and 1 percent of the loan to convert to a conventional loan without closing costs. Refinancing isn't just for ARMs, though.

Refinancing can also benefit people who have conventional loans. If interest rates have dropped since you bought your house, you should consider refinancing your loan. Whenever you refinance, you have to pay closing costs again, but the fee will be worth it if you plan to live in the house long enough to break even.

You can determine the number of months it will take you to break even by calculating your new principal and interest payment, and subtracting it from your current mortgage payment. That's your monthly savings. Then divide the closing costs by your savings.

Barry and Emily decided to test whether it was worth it to refinance their mortgage. They had a thirty-year $110,000 loan at 12 percent interest, but

Estimated Closing Costs Table

Loan Amount	Closing Costs	Loan Amount	Closing Costs
$30,000	$1,100	$ 75,000	$1,750
35,000	1,200	80,000	1,800
40,000	1,250	85,000	1,900
45,000	1,300	90,000	1,950
50,000	1,375	95,000	2,000
55,000	1,450	100,000	2,100
60,000	1,525	105,000	2,250
65,000	1,600	110,000	2,400
70,000	1,650	115,000	2,600

since they had bought the house interest rates had dropped to 7.5 percent. Using the factors on page 228, and the closing costs in the table above, they performed the following calculations:

New principal and interest payment

110,000	÷	1,000	=	110	×	9.28	=	$1,020.80
Loan	÷	1,000	=	Loan per $1,000	×	Factor	=	Monthly payment

Months to break even on refinance

$1,131.90	−	$1,020.80	=	$111.10
Current principal and interest payment	−	New principal and interest payment	=	Monthly savings

$2,400	÷	$111.10	=	21
Closing costs		Savings		# Months to break even

Using the factor for a fifteen-year loan, Barry and Emily determined that their new payment would be $111 less than their current payment, and it would take twenty-one months to break even. In less than two years, they would free up $111 they could use to save for retirement or their children's college fund. They went ahead with their refinancing.

Plug in the numbers for your principal and interest payments to determine whether it's worth it for you to refinance your loan. You will need to refer to the factor chart on page 228 and the closing costs chart on page 233.

New principal and interest payment

$$\underline{\qquad} \div \underline{1,000} = \underline{\qquad} \times \underline{\qquad} = \underline{\qquad}$$

Loan $\div$ 1,000 = Loan per $1,000 $\times$ Factor = Monthly payment

Months to break even on refinance

_____	−	_____	= _____
Current principal and interest payment		New principal and interest payment	Monthly savings
_____	÷	_____	= _____
(Closing costs)		(Savings)	(# Months to break even)

Refinancing only makes sense if you are able to save on your interest payments. If you have a thirty-year mortgage at a competitive rate, don't refinance just to pay off your house in fifteen years. Instead, just include an extra principal payment every time you send in your mortgage check. This will reduce the total amount you owe, allowing you to pay off the loan more quickly and saving you money. See page 233 for more on how to achieve this.

How to Save While You Get the Most for Your Money

Buying a house is one of the largest purchases you will ever make. In addition to following the Financial Peace rule of real estate—buy less house at lower rates over less time—you can be sure you are getting the most for your money and avoiding unnecessary expenses when you heed these tips:

- *Buy a used home instead of a new one.* You'll get more square footage and a better buy.
- *Buy a house that* can *be attractive.* Potential is everything. Bad landscaping, such as overgrown bushes, ugly carpet, flecked avocado green wallpaper, and the Elvis print in the bedroom can all become negotiating points—reasons for the owner to lower his price. Those are also characteristics of a home that can be fixed. What you *don't* want to buy is a poorly built, architecturally ugly house, one that needs a new foundation or face. Structural problems will come back to haunt you when you try to resell the house.
- *Buy a good floor plan.* Just because a house is big doesn't mean the space is used well. Some houses have as much as sixty to eighty square feet of wasted space, such as in a corner where you can't put anything. As you walk through the house, notice whether there is a wall to put the couch on or space to put the bed without covering a window.
- *Buy a house near water or with a view.* Aesthetics are everything when you are trying to sell a house, so buy a house in an attractive area. Avoid buying a house that overlooks an electrical plant or that is near an airport where the planes travel overhead every evening. In fact, it may be helpful to visit the neighborhood at several different times of day to observe the traffic on the street, whether there are families out in the yards, and what kind of noise pollution is in the area.
- *Get preapproved.* Preapproval gives you the power of a cash buyer when it comes to negotiating the price of a home. That's because the owner knows you can close quickly, within five to ten days, once you find a

235

house. So before you start seriously looking at houses, have a lender do the necessary paperwork—including pulling verifications of employment (VOEs) and verifications of deposit (VODs), and doing a detailed credit search—to approve you for a loan. You will have to pay $35 to $85 for your credit report, depending on where you live, but it will be worth it. After preapproval, the only step left to get a loan will be the property appraisal, which will cost about $345.

As you consider your home-buying options, take time to dream on paper. Make a list of what you are looking for in a house—first, the must-haves (e.g., two bathrooms), then the amenities you could live without if everything else were perfect (e.g., a deck). If you are married, have each spouse make a list on a separate sheet of paper. Then compare your lists and talk about what are your shared priorities and needs.

Must Have   **Negotiable**

_____   _____

_____   _____

_____   _____

_____   _____

_____   _____

Keep these lists with you. They can help when you are negotiating the price of a house. You may be able to talk a seller down on his price, for example, if he has everything but one of your must-haves.

Baby Step 6: Pay Off House Early

You begin taking the sixth baby step as soon as you sign the contract for your house. The goal is to pay it off earlier than the term of your mortgage. Ultimately, this goal will help prevent you from buying too much house and becoming house poor.

Wake-up Call! 🐓

The FDIC reports that 97.3 percent of people do not prepay any kind of debt systematically. You may say you will pay off that thirty-year loan in fifteen years, but you're lying to yourself. Go ahead and get the fifteen-year or less mortgage now.

Did you know that you can pay off a $100,000, thirty-year, 10 percent mortgage in twenty-two years, just by paying one extra payment per year? Take time now to create an action plan for paying off your house early by answering the following questions.

What are the terms of your loan?

_____

Call your mortgage banker and ask how much you owe on the house. By paying one extra payment per year, how long would it take to pay off your loan?

_____

Calculate in the space below how much more it would cost to make mortgage payments as if you had a fifteen-year note at the same interest. Refer to the loan factors chart on page 228.

_____ ÷ 1,000 = _____ × _____ = _____

Loan amount ÷ 1,000 = Price @ 1,000 ×   15-year   = New monthly payment
                                              loan factor

Now subtract the old monthly payment from the new to figure out how much extra you are going to have to earn to make the new monthly payment.

$$\underline{} \quad - \quad \underline{} \quad = \quad \underline{}$$

New monthly payment   –   Old monthly payment   =   Extra income

List ways you can cut back or earn more so you can pay one extra payment per year or pay your mortgage as if it were a fifteen-year note.

Expense	Amount

Hope for the Dream

The 1994 Fannie Mae–sponsored poll cited at the beginning of the chapter revealed a disturbing statistic: 65 percent of the survey participants said they were unable to make their home-ownership dream come true because they didn't have the necessary down payment and closing costs. That won't be the case for you if you take the baby steps out of debt and into saving money and building wealth. Instead, you will soon be able to afford not only a down payment and closing costs on a home but to pay off your home in fifteen years or less. What's more, you will be able to save to help your children buy their first home. At the least, you will be able to pass on to them a legacy of debt freedom and financial peace.

The Peace Track

Baby Step Checkup

Along the way, you will likely meet people who will advise you to keep your mortgage as long as you can and pay off your other debts slowly so you can save your cash. There will even be some who suggest that you *need* to carry debt. Those people have never been broke. What's more, they are likely living paycheck to paycheck.

Most people *do* carry debt, but they don't *need* to. Most people retire broke. Most people are living paycheck to paycheck. Most people are putting their kids through college with student loans. Do you want to do what *most people* are doing? I don't. Get out of debt if you haven't already. Get weird —normal is broke. Start saving for your retirement and your children's college. Then make it your goal to pay off the house early. Note how far you have come in completing these goals in the baby step checkup.

Baby Step	**Done**	**Action Needed to Complete**	**Date**
1. Save $1,000 in an emergency fund.			
2. Pay off all debt using the debt snowball.			
3. Complete your emergency fund by saving three to six months' expenses.			
4. Invest 15 percent of your gross household income in Roth IRAs and pretax retirement plans.			
5. Save for your kids' college education.			
6. Pay off your home early.			

People often call in to *The Money Game* radio show and say, "We have paid off our debts, even our house. Now what?" Take time this week to write some financial goals you would like to work on after you have paid off your house.

You may want to refer back to the ten- and twenty-year goals you recorded in chapter 8, page 139.

Weekly Goals

	Goal	Date
Spiritual		
Relational		
Physical		
Mental		

THIRTEEN

Leave a Legacy of Financial Peace

"I DON'T KNOW what to do now that we're out of debt," J. G. said one afternoon. "We're on a budget; we have just bought a house, which we're trying to pay off in ten to fifteen years. What's next?"

What's next after you finish paying off your house is the seventh and final baby step:

Build wealth and give like crazy.

That's right, go crazy getting rich! Now that you have no payments and a savings plan in place, you can grow your wealth for future generations by investing in real estate, more mutual funds, variable annuities (for the tax deferral), and other opportunities. While your investment money is multiplying on its own (remember compounding interest?), you can spend your time managing it, donating it to your family, your church, and worthy causes, and teaching sound financial principles to your children so they will wisely manage their own money.

Give Your Money Wisely

The itinerant pastor John Wesley said, "Make all you can; save all you can; give all you can." As you build your wealth, it's important that you use your money to benefit others. God made us with the need to give; it is essential for our spiritual, emotional, and even physical health. When you give of your time and money, your energy, creativity, and productivity increase. One client talked about the thrill of getting his finances under control and being able to reach out to help someone else. Another talked about the peace she felt during tough times because she continued giving despite her lack of funds.

If you haven't already made giving part of your budget, plan one way you can donate part of your income this week.

_____

_____

If you are really struggling financially, do what a friend suggested when I was going broke. Go serve soup to the homeless one evening. You will be helping others and keeping your own whining to a minimum. Take time to think of other ways you can give of your time. Have the whole family join you for this exercise.

_____

_____

For a directory of almost all national volunteer efforts, you can call Points of Light, in Washington, D.C., (202) 223-9186. Founded during President George Bush's administration, the organization serves as a clearinghouse for volunteering and matches individuals with volunteer efforts throughout the country.

Take time to set some long-term giving goals. List four causes that interest you, including your local church. (Again, have the whole family join you for this exercise.)

1. _____
2. _____
3. _____
4. _____

Now make it a goal to start giving a small percentage of your income to each of these organizations. If you are a Christian, you should be tithing, giving 10 percent of your income to the local church. The Scripture makes it clear that the tithe is God's provision for widows (and single mothers), orphans, and pastors. Steadily increase your giving as your financial situation improves.

As you consider where you will donate your time and money, remember, it's important that you give responsibly. That means you need to make sure the organizations you give to are legitimate. Here's how.

- *Legitimate organizations have open books.* Research the charitable organizations on your list. Call them up and ask to see a copy of their financial statements. If they won't tell you where their money goes, you shouldn't give to them.
- *Call the experts.* For general information, call the National Fraud Information Center at 1-800-876-7060, or contact the National Charities Information Bureau's Web site at http://www.give.org. For information about Christian organizations, contact Paul Nelson at the Evangelical Council for Financial Accountability (ECFA), at (703) 713-1414. These organizations track hundreds of charities' finances and what percentage of donations go to overhead.

After you have verified the legitimacy of the organizations on your list, narrow your choices to one organization. (You can donate to more causes later. Start with one.) Then decide an amount you can give, no matter how small, and try to give that for the next ninety days.

In addition to considering how you can use your money to benefit worthy causes, think about how you can use your money to help your family.

Take a moment to imagine what your children's lives would be like if they started their adult lives debt-free. If you could earn enough money, what would you want to help them fund? *(Example: graduate school, their first house, their own business.)*

1. _____

2. _____

3. _____

Take a moment to set some financial goals. How would you like your money to be distributed in your will? Write some goals below.

_____

_____

_____

_____

Talk about your goals with your spouse; make sure the two of you agree on your goals. Then, if you don't have a will already, make an appointment with an attorney and begin the process of estate planning.

Teach Your Children Well

"If only I had started saving and investing when I got my first job," Barry lamented one evening after one of his final FPU classes. "I envy J. G. and Jill and Dennis. They have their whole lives ahead of them."

"Hold on, Barry," Emily said, laughing. "We aren't in the grave yet. Sure, we could be further ahead than we are, but look at what we've learned. And look at what our kids are learning with us. Just the other day, Luke told me he would never have a credit card and he would never borrow money to buy a car. That tells me he's picked up something good from what we've been through."

When people start learning to control their finances, they often express regrets about "what could have been." "If only I had managed my money differently; if only I hadn't borrowed that $10,000, I could have . . ." Now isn't the time to rue the past. You have made your mistakes; you can't take them back. Remember Disney's *The Lion King*? When the lion cub Simba runs away, the wise old witch-doctor monkey has to find him and bring him back to be the king, but the cub doesn't want to come back. He doesn't think he is worthy to be king because of his past, so he protests the monkey's suggestion that he return to the kingdom. When he does, the monkey takes his cane and whacks him on the head.

"Ow! What'd ya do that for?" Simba asks.

"Doesn't matter. It's in the past," the monkey replies.

Your financial mistakes don't matter now. They are in the past. What does matter is that you learn from your mistakes and take time to pass on what you learn to future generations—your children.

In his book *How to Manage Your Money*, Larry Burkett describes a Jewish retirement tradition from biblical times. When a man retired, he gave all of his assets to his oldest male child (the oldest female if there were no sons) and made the son financially responsible for the son's parents and any un-married sisters until their death. If you knew you were going to have to depend on your child to provide a good lifestyle, food, shelter, and clothing during your twilight years, wouldn't you want to teach him well before you handed over the finances? It's important that you teach financial principles to your children as if your life depended on it.

Better Caught Than Taught

Your children are watching you. You have the formula for financial peace and success in your hands, and the kids are taking notes on what you are doing. That's because kids learn by example.

You've heard the saying "More lessons are caught than taught." You learn almost all of your money habits from your parents and television. Did your parents get a paycheck on Friday night and spend it by Monday morning? Or did they slave over the bills and balance the checkbook to the penny? It's likely that you picked up some of their traits, just by observation. Whatever they did, you took note and followed in their footsteps or rebelled and went in the opposite direction.

What financial habits did you pick up from your parents?

_____

_____

_____

_____

Have these lessons helped or hurt as you have dealt with your money?
How?

_____

_____

_____

_____

Now take a moment to consider what habits you would like your children to
pick up from you. List three in the space below:

1. _____

2. _____

3. _____

What, specifically, can you do to instill those habits in your children? Brainstorm ideas (with your spouse, if married), and record them below:

_____

_____

_____

_____

Practice Makes Perfect

Children also learn by experience, by putting ideas into action rather than
by simply talking about them. When kids are paid for household chores, for
example, they learn firsthand valuable financial lessons, such as "Work, get
paid; don't work, don't get paid." They gain confidence from the experience
of working, earning, saving, shopping, and finally purchasing a longed-for
item. You can also teach them lessons, such as giving to good causes and not
spending all you make.

When your kids turn three, you can start paying them a commission for
their work. Note: I didn't say pay them an "allowance." Children don't need
to grow up thinking someone has to make allowances for them. They can,

however, earn commissions for such tasks as putting away their toys and cleaning their rooms.

Use the worksheet on page 249 to set up a commission structure for your children's housework. Make a list of chores they can do and what each is worth. Then have them initial or place a sticker on each chore they do on the day they complete it. Hang it up where everyone can see it. That way the kids will have a reminder of their earning power. The worksheet Barry and Emily created for their kids is on page 248.

You may want to re-create the chart with space for more activities, or you may want to use the one on page 249. At the end of the week, add the total amount earned for the week, and pay each child.

Another way children can get firsthand money-management experience: Let them participate in the journey to financial peace. One woman who attended a Financial Peace University seminar started teaching her daughter about money when she was ten years old. By the time her daughter turned thirteen, she was doing the household budget and balancing the checkbook. You teach your kids how to behave, eat, cook, clean house, drive, bathe. Why not teach them how to handle money too? By the time they are ten or twelve years old, they have the necessary math skills to help reconcile the checkbook and plan the budget.

Make it a goal to call a family meeting once a month and discuss the family financial goals. Do you want to save money for a vacation? Ask your kids to share their savings goals. Solicit everyone's ideas for how the family can cut back on spending. You may decide to go to fewer movies and, instead, tape the family's favorite television shows so you can watch them together on weekends. Perhaps there is a home project, such as painting the house, that family members could pitch in and do together instead of hiring someone to do it. In addition to saving money, your children will learn the importance of giving and supporting the family.

Your family financial meetings should be mandatory for any family member five or older. Children five years old and younger may lose interest and not

Commission Worksheet

Date: March 3

Weekly Activity	Fee	Mon.	Tues.	Wed.	Thur.	Fri.	Sat.	Sun.	Total
Clean room for the week	$2.00								
Make bed each day	$1.00								
Fold laundry for the week	$1.00								
Empty trash each day	$1.00								
Weed garden, once a week	$3.00								
Mow lawn, once a week	$5.00								
Trim hedges, once a week	$4.00								

want to participate. That's okay. Here's an agenda for your first family financial meeting:

I. Open with prayer.
II. Review family budget.
    1. Go over clothing, food and blow money budgets, in particular.

Commission Worksheet

Date: _____

Activity	Fee	Mon.	Tues.	Wed.	Thur.	Fri.	Sat.	Sun.	Total

2. Answer questions, such as "Why can't I have $125 for new Nikes?" (You can answer these questions by showing the kids how paying for what they want will cut into savings and spending for college, retirement, groceries, etc.)
3. Talk about goals for savings and spending money earned this month.
4. Discuss changes in budget—where the family may have to cut back.

III. Talk about charitable giving.
  1. What causes are you supporting now?
  2. Are there other causes you want to support? Are there ways you can give of your time as well as your money?
IV. Discuss family projects.
 V. Final questions/complaints.
VI. Close with prayer.

The spirit of these meetings needs to be one of openness and honesty. Family members need to feel the freedom to ask questions and admit mistakes. If you come across as Herr Diktator, the kids will tune you out (especially teenagers) and everyone will learn to hate budgets and money management. If you keep reminding everyone (including yourself) that this is something the whole family is doing together so you can grow wealthy together, the meetings will go smoothly and everyone will want to participate.

Looking Back on the Peace Track

The last baby step is the first step on a road you'll be on for the rest of your life. Before you move forward, turn around and look back. Take a moment to consider how far you have come taking the first six baby steps and answer the following questions:

Do you have three to six months' expenses saved in your emergency fund?

_____

If not, imagine what it will be like to have at least $10,000 saved just for emergencies. How would that feel?_____

How much do you still owe on the debt snowball?_____

Shut your eyes and imagine what it will feel like to have no debt. Describe your feelings below.

_____

_____

What is it like knowing you are funding your retirement every month?

_____

_____

What will it be like to have your kids' college funded monthly?

_____

_____

What will it be like having your insurance in place, knowing your family is protected from financial disaster (barring a worldwide economic collapse)?

_____

_____

What will it be like to give consistently and generously to your church and other worthy causes?

_____

_____

The seven financial baby steps have put you on the road to financial peace. They guarantee a financially secure retirement and the joy of knowing you have provided for yourself and your family. If you have skipped any of the steps, go back in the workbook and do them now. Skipping steps gives you financial shin splints. You will wind up flat on the track, massaging your sore, empty checkbook and wondering where you went wrong.

You won't be able to do everything in this workbook perfectly. You may slip up every now and then. But even if you blow your budget one month, make sure you stick to it the next month. If you couldn't save last month, save this month. Remember, even a 25 percent improvement in each area will change your life dramatically. And one day you will suddenly realize that you have gotten control of your finances, and you will start to have *fun!*

The Peace Track

As you plan your goals for the week, take time to read and think about the following verses from the Book of Proverbs.

Give up trying so hard to get rich.
Your money flies away before you know it, just like an eagle suddenly taking off. (23:4–5)

If you are managing your money well, you won't have to try as hard to get rich. Take time to think how sound financial management might relieve you of some of the stress of working hard to "get rich."

_____

_____

_____

_____

Train up a child in the way he should go,
And when he is old he will not depart from it. (22:6)

How might this apply to teaching your children financial principles?

_____

_____

_____

_____

One of the habits I hope you continue after you finish this planner is making a list of weekly goals. Even better, try creating a list of goals for the month. Set aside time one night before the month begins when you will tackle this project and update your budget. Make a list of objectives; then, at the end of each week in the month, you can review your list and see how you are doing. At the end of the month, check the goals you are able to accomplish.

Take time now to create a list of your goals, or objectives, for next month.

To help remind you of your goals, keep this list where you can see it. Or take time to record the date you would like to accomplish these objectives on a calendar you keep where you will see it, such as on the refrigerator in the kitchen or on your desk in the study or at work.

Monthly Goals

	Goal	Date
Spiritual		
Relational		
Physical		
Mental		

Appendix A

Credit Cleanup

You can get a copy of your credit report by calling one of the following phone numbers for the national credit bureaus:

TRW Credit Bureau, 800-392-1122: One free copy per year; additional copies are $7 each.

Equifax Credit Bureau, 800-685-1111: Copies cost from $3 to $8.

TransUnion Credit Bureau, 800-916-8800: Personal credit file copies cost as much as $15, depending on the state where you live.

If the credit bureau will not cooperate in cleaning up your credit report, you can contact the FTC national headquarters or one of the regional FTC offices:

Federal Trade Commission National Headquarters
(202) 326-2222
6th and Pennsylvania Avenue, NW
Washington, D.C. 20580
For help cleaning up a credit bureau report, financial counseling, or credit-related counseling, you can call one of the following sources:

Bankcard Holders of America, (540) 389-5445: Offers support services, including mediation in cardholder and issuer disputes, for credit card holders. Dues are $24 a year.

Federal Trade Commission, (202) 452-3245: Publishes a brief list on card pricing by the largest credit card issuers. Copies are $5 and are published twice a year, in March and September. Also offers several free credit-related publications.

NFCC/Consumer Credit Counseling Services, 800-388-CCCS: A non-profit organization providing support services for credit card holders needing assistance managing their credit.

NCFE/National Center for Financial Education, P.O. Box 34070, San Diego, California 92163: A nonprofit organization that provides financial educational services for consumers. Produces a number of publications, including "Do-It-Yourself Credit Repair and Improvement Guide" for $10.

National Consumers League, (202) 835-3323: Call for publication on credit-related issues.

Consumer Insurance Information

You can reach your state insurance department by calling one of the following numbers:

Alabama: (205) 269-3550	Hawaii: (808) 586-2790
Alaska: (907) 465-2515	Idaho: (208) 334-2250
Arizona: (602) 912-8400	Illinois: (217) 782-4515
Arkansas: (501) 686-2900	Indiana: (317) 232-2385
California: (916) 445-5544	Iowa: (515) 281-5705
Colorado: (303) 894-7499	Kansas: (913) 296-7801
Connecticut: (203) 297-3800	Kentucky: (502) 564-3630
Delaware: (302) 739-4251	Louisiana: (504) 342-5900
Florida: (904) 922-3100	Maine: (207) 582-8707
Georgia: (404) 656-2056	Maryland: (410) 333-6200
Guam: (671) 477-5144	Massachusetts: (617) 727-3357

Michigan: (517) 373-9273

Minnesota: (612) 296-6848

Mississippi: (601) 359-3569

Missouri: (314) 751-2640

Montana: (406) 444-2040

Nebraska: (402) 471-2201

Nevada: (702) 687-4270

New Hampshire: (603 271-2261

New Jersey: (609) 292-5363

New Mexico: (505) 827-4500

New York: (212) 602-0203

North Carolina: (919) 733-7349

North Dakota: (701) 224-2440

Ohio: (614) 644-2658

Oklahoma: (405) 521-0071

Oregon: (503) 378-4271

Pennsylvania: (717) 787-5173

Puerto Rico: (809) 722-8686

Rhode Island: (401) 277-2223

South Carolina: (803) 737-6160

South Dakota: (605) 773-3563

Tennessee: (615) 741-2241

Texas: (512) 463-6464

Utah: (801) 538-3800

Vermont: (802) 828-3301

Virginia: (804) 371-9741

Virgin Islands: (809) 774-2991

Washington: (206) 753-7301

West Virginia: (304) 558-3394

Wisconsin: (608) 266-0102

Wyoming: (307) 777-7401

For more information call the National Insurance Consumer Helpline (NICH) at 800-942-4242.

Appendix B

Your Equity Sheet

ITEM/Describe	Value	–	Debt	=	Equity
Real Estate_____	_____	–	_____	=	_____
Real Estate_____	_____	–	_____	=	_____
Car_____	_____	–	_____	=	_____
Car_____	_____	–	_____	=	_____
Cash on Hand	_____	–	_____	=	_____
Checking Account 1	_____	–	_____	=	_____
Checking Account 2	_____	–	_____	=	_____
Savings Account 1	_____	–	_____	=	_____
Savings Account 2	_____	–	_____	=	_____
Money Market Account	_____	–	_____	=	_____
Mutual Funds	_____	–	_____	=	_____
Retirement Plan	_____	–	_____	=	_____
Stocks or Bonds	_____	–	_____	=	_____
Cash Value Insurance	_____	–	_____	=	_____
Household Items	_____	–	_____	=	_____
Jewelry	_____	–	_____	=	_____
Antiques	_____	–	_____	=	_____

Continued on next page

Boat	_____	−	_____	=	_____
Unsecured Debt (Negative)	_____	−	_____	=	_____
Credit Card Debt (Negative)	_____	−	_____	=	_____
Other_____	_____	−	_____	=	_____
Other_____	_____	−	_____	=	_____
Other_____	_____	−	_____	=	_____
TOTAL	_____	−	_____	=	_____

Your Income Sources

Source	Amount	Period/Describe
Salary 1	_____	_____
Salary 2	_____	_____
Salary 3	_____	_____
Bonus	_____	_____
Self-employment	_____	_____
Interest Income	_____	_____
Dividend Income	_____	_____
Royalty Income	_____	_____
Rents	_____	_____
Notes	_____	_____
Alimony	_____	_____
Child Support	_____	_____
AFDC	_____	_____
Unemployment	_____	_____
Social Security	_____	_____
Pension	_____	_____
Annuity	_____	_____
Disability Income	_____	_____
Cash Gifts	_____	_____
Trust Fund	_____	_____

Continued on next page

Other	_____			_____
Other	_____			_____
Other	_____			_____
TOTAL	_____			_____

Your Monthly Cash-Flow Plan

Category	Budgeted	Subtotal	% Take-Home	Amount Spent
Charitable Gifts	_____			_____
		_____	_____	_____
Savings				
Emergency Fund	_____			_____
Retirement Fund	_____			_____
College Fund	_____			_____
		_____	_____	_____
Housing				
First Mortgage	_____			_____
Second Mortgage	_____			_____
Real Estate Taxes	_____			_____
Homeowners Insurance	_____			_____
Home Repairs	_____			_____
Replace Furniture	_____			_____
Other_____	_____			_____
		_____	_____	
Utilities				
Electricity	_____			_____
Water	_____			_____
Gas	_____			_____
Phone	_____			_____
Trash	_____			_____
Cable	_____			_____
Computer On-line	_____			_____
		_____		_____

Continued on next page

Food
    Grocery   _____   _____
    Restaurants   _____   _____

Transportation
    Car Payment 1   _____   _____
    Car Payment 2   _____   _____
    Gas and Oil   _____   _____
    Repairs and Tires   _____   _____
    Car Insurance   _____   _____
    License and Taxes   _____   _____
    Car Replacement   _____   _____

Clothing
    Children   _____   _____
    Adults   _____   _____
    Cleaning/Laundry   _____   _____

Medical/Health
    Disability Insurance   _____   _____
    Health Insurance   _____   _____
    Doctor Bills   _____   _____
    Dentist   _____   _____
    Optometrist   _____   _____
    Drugs   _____   _____
    Other_____   _____   _____

Personal
    Life Insurance   _____   _____
    Child Care   _____   _____
    Baby-sitter   _____   _____
    Toiletries   _____   _____
    Hair Care   _____   _____

Continued on next page

Personal (*cont.*)
　　Education/Adult _____　　　　　　　_____
　　School Tuition _____　　　　　　　_____
　　School Supplies _____　　　　　　　_____
　　Child Support _____　　　　　　　_____
　　Alimony _____　　　　　　　_____
　　Subscriptions _____　　　　　　　_____
　　Organization Dues _____　　　　　　　_____
　　Gifts (Christmas) _____　　　　　　　_____
　　Miscellaneous _____　　　　　　　_____

Blow $$ _____　_____ _____　　_____

Recreation
　　Entertainment _____　　　　　　　_____
　　Vacation _____　　　　　　　_____

Debts ($0, you hope)
　　Visa 1 _____　　　　　　　_____
　　Visa 2 _____　　　　　　　_____
　　MasterCard 1 _____　　　　　　　_____
　　MasterCard 2 _____　　　　　　　_____
　　American Express _____　　　　　　　_____
　　Discover Card _____　　　　　　　_____
　　Gas Card 1 _____　　　　　　　_____
　　Gas Card 2 _____　　　　　　　_____
　　Dept. Store Card 1 _____　　　　　　　_____
　　Dept. Store Card 2 _____　　　　　　　_____
　　Finance Co. 1 _____　　　　　　　_____
　　Finance Co. 2 _____　　　　　　　_____
　　Credit Line _____　　　　　　　_____
　　Student Loan 1 _____　　　　　　　_____
　　Student Loan 2 _____　　　　　　　_____

Debts (*cont.*)

    Other_____ _____   _____

    Other_____ _____   _____

    Other_____ _____   _____

GRAND TOTAL   _____   _____   _____

−TOTAL INCOME   _____   _____

ZERO   _____   _____

Notes

Chapter 1. Call Me Weird—Just Don't Call Me Broke

6. *According to* Consumer . . . : Jeff Blyskal, "Loans," *The Consumer Reports Money Book* (New York: Consumers Union of the United States, 1995), p. 32.

6. *Seventy percent of . . .* : *Fast Facts on Consumer Credit Problems and Bankruptcy*, Dearborn Trade.

6. *And the 1996 . . .* : National Foundation for Consumer Credit, "New Study Reveals Say It Is More Difficult to Pay Bills Than Three Years Ago," July 22, 1996. For more information, call Consumer Credit Counseling Service at (800) 388-2227. Or visit the National Foundation for Consumer Credit Home Page at http://www.nicc.org.

10. *Most couples cite . . .* : Robert Sullivan, "Americans and Their Money: An Intimate Portrait," *Worth*, June 1994, p. 60.

Chapter 2. What's a Nice Guy Like You Doing in a Place Like This?

18. *Studies vary, but . . .* : David Morrow, "To Shop, Perchance Nonstop," *New York Times*, December 29, 1996, F-1, p. 12.

Chapter 3. "Budget" by Another Name—May Help

29. *When Drs. Thomas . . .* : Thomas J. Stanley, Ph.D., and William D. Danko, Ph.D., *The Millionaire Next Door: The Surprising Secrets of America's Wealth* (Atlanta: Longstreet Press, 1996), p. 40.

Chapter 5. What Kind of Debt Have You Bought?

86. *Dennis believed Visa . . .* : "Consumer Debt Issue," *CardTrak*, February 27, 1997 (Frederick, Maryland: RAM Research).

87. *While banks and . . . :* "The Largest Issuers of Bank Credit Cards," *CardTrak*, July 1995, p. 11 (Frederick, Maryland: RAM Research).

87. *At the rate . . . :* "Credit Daze," *Smart Money*, March 1995, p. 76.

87. *In 1996, the . . . :* "Fed Interest Rate Hike: Cardholders Will Eat It," *CardTrak*, September 23, 1996 (Frederick, Maryland: RAM Research).

87. *And personal bankruptcies . . . :* Fred Vogelstein, "Giving Credit Where Credit Is Undue," *U.S. News & World Report*, March 31, 1997, p. 52.

88. *That year, Americans . . . :* Anne Willette, "GM Card Ringing Up Food Rebates," *USA Today*, n.d.

88. *According to the . . . :* "Credit Cards," *Consumer Reports*, January 1996.

88. *Seventy-two percent of . . . :* "Credit Daze," *Smart Money*, March 1995, p. 76.

89. *Home equity loans . . . :* Phillip Fiorini, "Lenders Offer Incentives on Equity Loans," *USA Today*, March 13, 1995, p. B-5.

91. *According to* Consumer . . . : "Or Should You Lease Instead?" *Consumer Reports*, April 1994, p. 259.

97. *You may remember . . . :* Bobby Eklund and Terry Austin, *Partners with God! Bible Truths About Giving* (Nashville, Tenn.: Convention Press, 1994).

Chapter 6. Reversal of Fortune: Dump Debt

101. *Seventy-eight percent of . . . :* RAM Research Group (Frederick, Maryland).

101. *Consumers spend 12 percent . . . :* "When to Borrow, When to Pay Cash," *Dun and Bradstreet Reports*, March/April 1993, p. 63.

Chapter 7. Credit Cleanup

114. *The act makes . . . :* Federal Trade Commission, Bureau of Consumer Protection, Office of Consumer & Business Education, *Facts for Consumers*, September 1992. For more information, write Federal Trade Commission, Washington D.C. 20580. Or call (202)326-3650.

Chapter 8. Show Me the Money: Make Compound Interest Work for You

129. *According to a . . . :* "Financial Planning 101," *Money*, March 1989, p. 12.

142. *Usually the wealthy . . . :* Thomas J. Stanley, Ph.D., and William D. Danko, Ph.D., *The Millionaire Next Door: The Surprising Secrets of America's Wealth* (Atlanta: Longstreet Press, 1996), p. 3.

Chapter 9. Spread It Around: The Power of Diversification

152. *According to one . . . :* John R. Dorfman, "Toss of the Darts Bests Pros in Stock-Picking Contest," *Wall Street Journal*, July 1993, p. C-1.

Chapter 10. To Everything There Is a Season: College and Retirement

163. *According to a Gallup . . . :* Dennis Kelly, "Parents Believe in College but Don't Have the Cash," *USA Today*, September 20, 1996, p. 1.

163. *According to* Forbes . . . *:* Dana Wechsler, "Where's Your 1.25 Million?" *Forbes*, June 21, 1993, p. 176.

163. *As a whole . . . :* Anne Willette, "Poll: Only 44% Are Preparing for Retirement," *USA Today*, May 8, 1995, p. 1.

164. *A December 30 . . . :* Anne Willette, "Wall Street, Workers Key to Solvency," *USA Today*, December 30, 1996, p. B-1.

164. *What's more, the . . . :* "But Money Is Still a Problem for Every Consumer," U.S. Census Bureau, 1984 Current Population Survey.

164. *In their book . . . :* Thomas J. Stanley, Ph.D., and William D. Danko, Ph.D., *The Millionaire Next Door: The Surprising Secrets of America's Wealth* (Atlanta: Longstreet Press, 1996), p. 16.

165. Fortune *magazine says . . . :* James Alvey, "Skimpy Savings," *Fortune*, February 20, 1995.

178. *According to the Gallup . . . :* Dennis Kelly, "Parents Believe in College but Don't Have the Cash," *USA Today*, September 20, 1996, p. 1.

178. *The increase in . . . :* Karen W. Arenson, "Tuitions Rising at a Faster Rate Than Inflation," *New York Times*, September 26, 1996, p. 1.

181. *According to the College . . . :* "1996–97 Increase in College Costs Averages Five Percent; Student Financial Aid at Record High," College Board, September 25, 1996. *The College Board Annual Survey of Colleges, 1996* reports tuition and fees for the current academic year, 1996–97. For more information, visit the *College Board Online*.

Chapter 11. Protect Your Investments—and Your Loved Ones: Insurance

188. *According to the . . . :* "Insurance," *Worth Solution Series*, Capital Publishing Limited Partnership, 1995.

191. *In his book . . . :* Michael Harry Minton, *What Is a Wife Worth?* cited in "Real Men *Do* Vacuum," *Aspire*, May 1996, p. 34.

199. *Your chances of . . . :* "Insurance," *Worth Solution Series*, Capital Publishing Limited Partnership, 1995.

204. *Other ways to . . . :* Insurance Information Institute, "12 Ways to Lower Your Homeowners Insurance." For a free brochure, send a self-addressed, stamped envelope to 110 William Street, New York, New York 10038. Call (212)669-9200 for more information.

209. *In fact, the average . . . :* "Are You Paying Too Much for Auto Insurance?" *Consumer Reports*, January 1997, p. 10.

211. *Some types of . . . :* "Are You Paying Too Much for Auto Insurance?" *Consumer Reports*, January 1997, p. 13.

215. *You can also . . . :* "Are You Paying Too Much for Auto Insurance?" *Consumer Reports*, January 1997, p. 13.

Chapter 12. To Buy or What to Buy? Real Estate and Mortgages

220. *According to a Federal National* . . . : "Who Wants to Own?" FNMA survey, May 16, 1995.
231. *According to the FDIC* . . . : Ellen DePasquale, "Mind Your Mortgage," *Worth*, February 1996.
238. *The 1994 Fannie* . . . : "Who Wants to Own?" Fannie Mae survey, May 16, 1995.

Chapter 13. Leave a Legacy of Financial Peace

245. *In his book* . . . : Larry Burkett, *How to Manage Your Money* (Chicago: Moody Press, 1975).

Appendix A

256. *You can reach* . . . : Insurance Information Institute, "Homeowners Insurance." For a free brochure, send a self-addressed, stamped envelope to 110 William Street, New York, New York 10038. Call (212)669-9200 for more information.

Index

THE

Money

GAME

Hosted by Dave Ramsey
"Money Talk with an Attitude"

Dave Ramsey's nationally syndicated
radio talk show, *The Money Game,*
is one of the fastest-growing and most
highly rated talk shows in the nation!

Hear and talk to Dave Ramsey as he answers
your financial questions each Monday
through Friday from 1 to 4 P.M. CST.

If you would like to learn how you can help bring
The Money Game to your area, call our office at
1-888-22PEACE. For a list of our affiliates,
browse our Web site at www.financialpeace.com.

The number one cause of divorce is money problems.
This important and inspiring road map will build wealth
while strengthening your marriage and family.

MORE THAN ENOUGH
The Proven Keys to Strengthening Your Family and Building Financial Peace

In his newest work, Dave Ramsey reveals the ten key traits that are essential to creating prosperity in your relationships, and in your wallet. Filled with the stories of couples, widows and widowers, single parents, children, and single men and women, *More Than Enough* will show you: how to achieve marital harmony through money; why living debt-free allows you to build wealth and change your family tree forever; what you need to teach your children about finances; how to avoid having the number one cause of divorce—money—destroy your marriage; and much, much more. Dave Ramsey's common-sense approach to life and finances will help you achieve personal control, life-time peace, and a new, vital family dynamic.

ISBN 0-670-88253-4

In his original bestseller, Dave Ramsey expounds the principles
that have helped so many regain control of their financial lives.

FINANCIAL PEACE
Restoring Financial Hope to You and Your Family

Whether you're facing a financial crisis or simply don't think your money is working hard enough for you, bestselling author Dave Ramsey offers tips on how to stay fiscally sound, deal with debt when the collector is at the door, and learn how to save money even when you think you can barely make ends meet. Dave uses a simple, common-sense approach to tackle a wide range of subjects including the absolute necessity of keeping a written budget, life insurance, mutual funds, and the power of cash. The sooner you implement Dave's advice in your own life, the sooner money can cease to be a worry and start to be an asset.

ISBN 0-140-26468-X